LIU YI AND THE DRAGON PRINCESS

Liu Yi and the Dragon Princess

A Thirteenth-Century *Zaju* Play
by Shang Zhongxian

Translated and Adapted by
David Hawkes

The Chinese University Press

Liu Yi and the Dragon Princess: A Thirteenth-Century Zaju *Play by Shang Zhongxian*
  Translated and Adapted by David Hawkes

© **The Chinese University of Hong Kong**, 2003

ISBN 962–996–064–8

THE CHINESE UNIVERSITY PRESS
The Chinese University of Hong Kong
SHA TIN, N.T., HONG KONG
Fax: +852 2603 6692
    +852 2603 7355
E-mail: cup@cuhk.edu.hk
Web-site: www.chineseupress.com

Printed in Hong Kong

To

Jacques and Sylvie

Contents

Acknowledgements

I should like to thank C. C. Liu and the other members of the Editorial Board of the Hong Kong Translation Society for permission to reprint the lyrics from *Liu Yi and the Dragon Princess* which were originally published in 2001 in the combined issue (Nos. 21 & 22) of their journal *The Translation Quarterly*.

I should also like to express my gratitude to the editorial and production staff of the Chinese University Press for their exemplary handling of the material printed in this little book at what must have been a very difficult time. In particular I should like to thank Esther Tsang for her unfailing encouragement and for the patience, skill and resourcefulness with which she has dealt with the frequent demands of a somewhat difficult author.

Introduction

This is an attempt — not too optimistic, I hope — to present an English version of a thirteenth-century Chinese music drama of the type called *zaju* which could be set to music and produced for performance on a Western stage.

Zaju was very popular during the so-called Yuan period (1276–1368) when China, dominated, like most of the rest of Asia, by the heirs of Genghis Khan, was ruled over by a dynasty of Mongol emperors. It gradually went out of fashion in the Ming period after the restoration of Chinese rule, though it continued to be patronised, often in a considerably modified form, by the conservative Imperial court until well into the sixteenth century. Today the music for it has virtually disappeared and the plays are never performed.

Zaju resembled comic opera or musical comedy in its mixture of song and spoken dialogue but differed in one important respect: only one of the actors sang throughout the entire performance, the rest had only speaking parts. Except for short prologues and interludes, which were in any case optional, nearly all *zaju* plays had four acts, each set to music in a different mode or key (the Chinese word means "tuning"), the music for all the lyrics or arias in an act being drawn from a repertoire of familiar tunes all in the same mode. The soloist, either male (*mo*) or female (*dan*), usually represented the same character throughout the play, but sometimes changed roles from one act to the other: for example, you could have a *zaju* in which the soloist sang the part of a man who got murdered in the first two acts and that of the detective who unmasked his murderer in the remaining half of the play.

About 160 Yuan *zaju* have survived, though the titles are known of very many more. The language they are written in, a vernacular Chinese slightly older than the English of Chaucer, is hard to understand, but even those who penetrate its difficulties with the help of footnotes and glossaries or who read *zaju* in translation are often disappointed if they are looking for tragic profundity, psychological insight or sparkling dialogue. The characters of *zaju*, whatever names they are given, are mostly stock characters like those of the old *commedia dell'arte*, the dialogue is childish or banal, and the dramatic interest lies entirely in the situations generated by the plot. What raises these dramas — the best of them at any rate — to the level of great literature and has ensured their survival despite centuries of non-performance and the loss of their music is the excellence of their lyrics — the parts of the play that were originally sung by the soloist. Though, from Da Ponte to Auden, European opera has had some distinguished librettists, no one thinks of operatic libretti as forming part of our literary heritage; yet that is exactly how educated Chinese think of Yuan *zaju*: as the most significant literary development of the Mongol century.

The playwrights who produced this lyrical drama could be described as unemployed poets who in better times might have hoped, like the young man in this play, to gain entry through the examination system to an administration which rewarded literary talent. Under the Mongol administration with its non-Chinese bias there were few satisfactions for gifted Chinese and supplying material for the entertainment industry became both an outlet for their talents and in some cases even a livelihood. Many of them organised themselves into writers' associations or guilds and some of their work was no doubt produced in collaboration.

The performers they wrote for included singers, actors, story-tellers and prostitutes. Many prostitutes were in fact trained as singers or instrumentalists and the line separating prostitutes from other sorts of entertainer was so vaguely drawn as to be almost non-existent. Most of the poet-playwrights were song-writers as well and some of them spent a great deal of their time with the talented inhabitants of the brothels for whom they wrote their songs. Nevertheless a social gulf existed between writers and entertainers. The status of actors and prostitutes was at the very bottom of the social scale whereas members of the writers' guilds who wrote plays and songs for them, even though some of them might be much less well-off than a successful actor-manager, were educated gentlemen and could command a certain amount of respect.

There is a *zaju* play dating from the Mongol period or slightly after about an actor-manager who owns one of the theatres in the amusement quarter of a large northern city. His troupe is quite a small one: himself, his wife, his son and daughter-in-law, two of his male cousins and a number of women musicians who can double for stage parts as need arises. He is himself a singer and the soloist in this play. We see him addressing his troupe at a little party given by them to celebrate his fiftieth birthday and referring in his speech to their indebtedness to the "kind gentlemen of the writers' guild" who supply them with the material on which to exercise their talents. We also get an idea of the lowly status of this successful and fairly prosperous man when he is summoned from the party, despite his pleas to be excused, to entertain some guests at the residence of the local magistrate and threatened with a flogging for not arriving more promptly when he complies. There was never any likelihood of a Chinese actor-manager writing his own plays and retiring at the end of his career to lead the life of a country gentleman as Shakespeare did a few centuries later in England.

The "*za*" of "*zaju*" means "mixed". *Zaju* are "mixed plays", the mixture being that of two pre-existing kinds of entertainment: buffooneries which consisted mostly of spoken dialogue between two or more comic actors, and solo performances in which a vocally accomplished story-teller alternated spoken narrative with lyrics set to tunes arranged in suites, each suite in a different mode or key. Most of the peculiarities of *zaju* can be accounted for by referring to this hybrid ancestry.

Chinese operatic drama developed out of story-telling and has always retained some of its story-telling characteristics. For example, you don't learn who a character is and what he is up to by listening to the dialogue: he faces the audience at his first appearance (and sometimes at his second, too, in case you've forgotten) and gives you his name, age and CV with full particulars, acting as his own narrator.

In two *zaju* plays the *zaju* playwright does in fact revert to pure narration. One is the sequence of lyrics in the second act of this play. They are sung by the *dan* soloist appearing not as the Dragon Princess, as she does in the other three acts, but as a messenger in the character of the Lightning Goddess, whose sole function is to tell the story of the Fire Dragon of Qiantang's battle with the son of the Dragon King of the Jing River. The device of the Messenger who describes actions which it would be impossible or inconvenient to show on the stage is a commonplace in Greek tragedy and one made much use of by Shakespeare, but not on the scale in which it is used here, where a whole act is devoted to it.

In the second example a *dan* soloist playing the role of a travelling ballad-singer reveals step by step, in a series of lyrics, the real identity of the young man she has been hired to entertain but whose nurse she had been when he was a child. In this case the sung lyrics, forming a long continuous narrative only interrupted by the spoken comments of the young man, constitute almost the whole of the last act.

The new interest taken by large numbers of poets and literary men in the theatre and their willingness to look to the theatre for their livelihood is only one of the reasons given for the sudden flowering of *zaju* in the Mongol period. An important contributory factor was the evolution of a new verse medium perfectly suited to the requirements of the stage which they could make use of in writing lyrics for their librettos.

Until modern times Chinese poetry was invariably in syllabic verse. This has to do with the nature of the Chinese language, in which, for example, the words for "horse", "monkey", "elephant" and "rhinoceros" are all monosyllables, making it possible to produce effects in Chinese verse which it is impossible to reproduce in English.

Until the tenth century most Chinese verse was written in lines of equal length — either five or seven syllables as a rule — though there was a growing tendency to vary the line-lengths when composing song-words, rather as Shakespeare uses regular metre in his sonnets but sometimes has stanza-patterns with lines of varying length in the songs which he inserts in his plays, like "Sigh no more ladies" or "You spotted snakes". From the tenth century onwards many Chinese poets began writing lyrics using stanza-patterns made up of lines of varying length sometimes with no intention of their being sung. The English "Metaphysical" poets like George Herbert and John Donne often used lyrical forms in the same way, simply because they found the patterns congenial.

The lyric style or "long-and-short verse" as it was sometimes called gave song-writers a certain amount of freedom, but since this was syllabic verse they still had to conform to a line of fixed length. The big breakthrough which Yuan *zaju*-writers exploited was the emergence, perhaps because of some musical development, of a kind of verse which conformed to the musical beat and yet allowed what were called "padding-words" outside the rhythm. It's a bit hard to demonstrate this in a language other than Chinese, but I'll attempt to do so.

Suppose you have a five-line stanza in which the rhythmic pattern is 7.7.3.3.7:

> **I am cold my feet are sore**
> **Do not turn me from your door**
> > **Pi-ty me**
> > **Let me in**
> **I'll be grate-ful e-ver-more**

By introducing padding-words you can if you wish greatly enlarge the length of the line, which gives you far greater freedom of expression:

> Please hear me **I am cold** so cold **my feet are sore**
> > I beg you **Do not** turn oh please don't **turn me from your**
> > **door**

> Kind lady **Pi-ty me** oh pity
> **Let me in**
> I swear that **I'll be grate-ful** e-ver-more

The word used for this new kind of lyric was *qu*. Rather
confusingly this word *qu* had long been in use in the sense of "tune",
but now it was used not only for this new kind of lyric, whether written
as a single number or part of a short song-cycle, but for the lyrics in
longer, elaborately constructed dramatic narratives and for the lyrics in
zaju. Sometimes it was even used of the *zaju* plays themselves. The
name which was given by its seventeenth-century editor to what is still
the most popular collection of *zaju* plays was "A Selection of Yuan
Qu".

The texts of the thirty *zaju* which are the only ones to have survived
in a contemporary Yuan edition do in fact contain little more than the
arias. The only spoken words given are those of the soloist, the words
of the other characters being omitted with only a brief indication that
somebody says something or that there is some dialogue or some
business or other at this point. In some cases even the words spoken by
the soloist are omitted.

Who had these plays printed? Was it the actor-manager, probably
himself the soloist? Or the playwright or some other member of the
writers' guild? In either case the spoken dialogue could not have been
thought particularly important by the people who bought the printed
copies. They may, of course, have wanted the copies as rather expensive programme-notes to enable them to follow the singing (in opera
it's nearly always hard to make out what the words are that are being
sung, whatever language they're being sung in) but I doubt this. I don't
think there's any evidence to suggest that people ever listened to opera
with a text. More likely they wanted the text to read later and remind
them of what they had been hearing, or so that they could learn the
words and sing them for themselves. At all events, it was the arias, the
qu, that interested them, not the dialogue.

For full texts of the *zaju* plays giving the whole of the spoken dialogue as well as the arias sung by the soloists we have to turn to late Ming editions, none of them earlier than 1588. Unfortunately there are signs that the words are not always the words that were used by the original Yuan performers. Some may have been altered or added to by the Ming editors and some may have been written by (or for) the actors of the Ming imperial court, the source from which the Ming editors got many of their texts.

It's also quite possible that there never *were* complete Yuan texts of the spoken dialogue. The actors may have extemporised a good deal, as they no doubt would have done in the earlier buffooneries, and they may have learned much of the dialogue and business by word of mouth (no doubt altering it from time to time to suit the needs of production) only relying on a few jotted notes to remind them of those passages in which they needed to be word-perfect. For instance, they would have needed some record of the doggerel verses they recited as they were making their entrances, particularly as these were made in full view of the audience and may sometimes have involved quite a bit of walking. They were usually stock verses suited to a particular type of character — old woman, innkeeper, dim-witted magistrate, and so forth — and could be used interchangeably in different plays. There were also occasionally little songs or poems to be sung or recited by players other than the soloist. These too would have had to be recorded for future reference.

The Yuan *zaju* plays were written for a commercial theatre. They catered for audiences which included the shopkeepers, traders, artisans, low-grade government employees and providers of various services who congregated in China's major cities, which were vastly bigger and more prosperous than any European city of the same period. Many of them may have been literate but not sufficiently educated to understand the finer points of the lyrics — which only a minority of the audience, members of the scholar class in hats and long gowns, would have appreciated — and would have derived more pleasure from the knockabout stuff provided by the clowns and the other speaking parts, only getting the general drift of what was being sung by the soloist.

Nevertheless even when showing off their learning in the lyrics, the gentlemen of the writers' guilds never lost sight of the fact that they were writing for a plebeian audience. For their plots they drew on the inexhaustible store of historical, religious, supernatural and romantic themes already exploited by story-tellers and ballad-singers, as well as on the more highbrow literature of the past; but they also wrote many *zaju* on contemporary themes in which the heroes and heroines were often fairly humble folk like the ones who constituted a large section of their audience. Government officials were often represented as stupid, corrupt or cruel (or all of these things); and even plays with a religious theme had more often than not to do with a very popular salvationist religion which many of their audience may have believed in.

Quanzhen ("Perfect Truth") Taoism, as it is usually called, was founded in the last quarter of the twelfth century by a crazed exciseman from north-west China. It was really not so much a form of Taoism as a mishmash of several religions: popular Taoism, Buddhism, Confucianism and Manichaeism. Its leaders, like the "Perfecti" among the Cathars of the West, were peripatetic and practised extreme austerity, renouncing private property and abstaining from meat, fish, alcohol and sex. As much as possible they even tried to do without sleep.

One of the founder's principal disciples won great power and prestige for the sect by travelling across Central Asia in his seventies and expounding its doctrines to Genghis Khan. He did not succeed in converting the Khan but impressed him so much that on his return to north China he was given a considerable say in Chinese religious affairs. Rather like the Salvation Army in the last century, the sect was famous for its charitable work among the poor and afflicted. For example, they reconstructed war-ruined Buddhist temples and (to the great indignation of the Buddhist orders) converted them into Quanzhen hospices; and they funded the ransoming and repatriation of hundreds of prisoners of war. This must have endeared them to ordinary people; but what made them a particularly attractive subject for the Yuan playwright was the dramatic nature of their conversions, which were always violent and sometimes terrifying.

In the *zaju* plays about Quanzhen conversions the object of the evangelist's attentions is usually a person of lowly status — a pedlar, a clerk, a prostitute, or an actor like the actor-manager in the play I mentioned above — who is, unknown to himself (or herself), an immortal spirit, banished to the earth for some infraction of the celestial code. These people could only be "saved" by being made to realise who they really were; and according to Quanzhen theory they could only be made to realise who they really were by undergoing some devastating trauma — or, if necessary, a whole series of them.

There was a strong supernatural element in all of these plays, because Quanzhen devotees believed in a whole lineage of spiritual ancestors stretching back before the time of their founder. Some of these were figures borrowed from Chinese folklore, but all were thought of as historical personages who had been transformed, by celestial favour or their own efforts, into Immortals.

"Liu Yi and the Dragon Princess" is about the supernatural, but it has nothing to do with Quanzhen or any other religious ideas. It is a late thirteenth-century dramatisation by the Yuan playwright Shang Zhongxian of a short story by the eighth-century Tang scholar Li Chaowei.

Li Chaowei's "The Story of Liu Yi" belongs to a class of tales, elegantly written in a slightly archaic prose style and often on supernatural or romantic themes (in this case both), which became very popular among educated people during the latter half of the Tang period (618–907). They seem to have originated as part of a portfolio that candidates for the civil service examination submitted to the examiners to demonstrate their virtuosity in prose and verse and their ability to construct a good narrative.

Shang Zhongxian shows every sign of having read the actual text of "The Story of Liu Yi". The two songs sung at the Dragon King's party in Act Three are lifted word for word from it, though he has switched them between the two singers, giving Lord Qiantang's song to Lord Dongting and vice versa. But it's rather hard to know just how much he intended to alter the plot of the story in his dramatisation of it, because sometimes the words of his lyrics don't square with the spoken parts of the play. For example, two of the lyrics refer to the Qiantang dragon's being chained to a pillar somewhere in Lord Dongting's palace and of his breaking out with the broken pillar trailing behind him when he hears of his niece's plight. This exactly accords with what is said in the story. But the spoken dialogue has him strolling over to the palace in human form, eavesdropping on what his brother says' about the Princess while pretending to have withdrawn to another room, and informing the audience that he is going off to mobilise his troops for battle before walking off the scene in human form.

Given the limitations of contemporary *zaju* theatre, it's understandable that the actors may have thought a scene showing a dragon flying off with a chain and a piece of pillar attached to it would be much too difficult to stage; but in that case why didn't the playwright alter the text of the play to remove the discrepancy between lyrics and dialogue? After all, he did avoid the difficulty of showing an aerial battle between two dragons by describing it in the series of lyrics given to the soloist which takes up much of Act Two, even though in the section just preceding it there is a passage of spoken dialogue which seems to have been written for the staging of a rather different version of the battle.

I think the answer must be that most of the spoken parts of the play weren't, in any case, written by the playwright but were left to the discretion of the actors. Half the audience probably couldn't understand the lyrics anyway and would have depended on the action and dialogue in order to follow the plot. In the following pages I shall try, by comparing a greatly abridged version of Li Chaowei's story with a synopsis of the full Ming text of Shang Zhongxian's *zaju*, to give some idea of the way in which the Yuan librettist's adaptation of the Tang story was further modified by the actors.

🁢   🁢   🁢   🁢

Liu Yi Zhuan

In the Yi-feng period (676–678) a young Hunanese scholar called Liu Yi was leaving the imperial capital after failing in the civil service examination when he remembered that a fellow-countryman of his was working in nearby Jingyang and decided to make a detour and call on him before returning to his home in Xiangyin. As he was riding along beside the Jing river a flock of birds suddenly flew up in front of him and his horse took fright and bolted, not stopping until it had galloped for at least a couple of miles out of his way.

When it finally halted, he found himself in a desolate stretch of the riverside where a young woman was minding a flock of sheep. She was strikingly beautiful, but she looked ill and was extremely poorly dressed. As she stood there, she appeared to be listening out for something. Liu Yi dismounted and politely inquired whether she was in trouble of some kind. At first she declined to answer, but then burst into tears.

She said she was the youngest daughter of the Dragon King of Lake Dongting, married by her parents to the younger son of the Dragon King of the River Jing. Her husband was a libertine, corrupted and enslaved by his male and female servants, who abused and maltreated her, but his indulgent parents refused to believe her when she complained and finally punished her by sending her to mind sheep beside the river. She seemed to have preternatural knowledge that Liu Yi came from an area near her old home, and asked him if he would consider taking a letter for her to her parents.

Liu Yi chivalrously declared that he would willingly do anything to help her, but doubted whether, as a mere mortal, he would be able to penetrate to the watery dragon-world of the Dongting Lake, whereupon the Princess told him about a great orange-tree that grew on the lakeside which he was to strike three times with his belt. This was the magic pass which would summon a guide who would take him to her father's kingdom. Liu Yi then promised to deliver the letter.

Before taking leave of her, he could not forbear asking her what dragon spirits were doing with sheep. Surely they didn't eat meat like human beings? The Princess said they weren't really sheep but rain-workers used by the dragons in manufacturing the weather. Liu Yi, as he looked at them, thought they seemed just like ordinary sheep, but when, shortly after leaving her, he glanced back again, both they and the Princess had vanished.

After visiting his friend, Liu Yi spent the next month travelling to his home in Hunan. He found the orange-tree on the shore of the lake that the Princess had told him of and when he struck it with his belt a warrior appeared from the water and transported him in a few instants to a room in the Dragon King's palace beneath the lake. The Dragon King, who had been listening to a Taoist sermon in a different part of the palace, appeared shortly after Liu Yi's arrival, received him graciously and took the letter. He read it with signs of grief and shock and reproached himself bitterly for his daughter's plight. Recovering himself a little, he thanked Liu Yi for his kindness in bringing the letter and handed it to a eunuch to take to the Queen and the other ladies in the inner apartments.

Presently sounds of lamentation could be heard from within and the King sent an urgent message asking the ladies to restrain themselves in case the sound of their grieving should provoke Lord Qiantang. Liu Yi inquired curiously who this Lord Qiantang was and why was it so important that he should not hear about the Princess. The Dragon King replied that Lord Qiantang was his younger brother, originally Dragon King of the River Qiantang but now, on the Celestial Emperor's orders, imprisoned in the palace because of various natural disasters he had caused in the past by his impetuous and violent behaviour.

Just as he was speaking there was an almighty roar, a deafening crash, and a huge red dragon appeared and flew off trailing a broken pillar from a long chain fastened round its neck. Liu Yi threw himself to the ground in terror and had to be lifted up and comforted by the King. He asked to be allowed to go home, but the King insisted that he stayed and assured him that his brother would not show himself as a dragon when he returned. Liu Yi was eventually persuaded to stay and for some time sat drinking with the King.

They were still drinking together when the music of flutes carried on a gust of perfumed air heralded the arrival of a bevy of maidens, presently followed by a young lady of dazzling beauty, gorgeously dressed and glittering with jewels, whom Liu Yi identified as the shepherd-girl he had met a month earlier beside the river.

"The prisoner of the River Jing has returned," said the Dragon King, as she passed with her maidens into the inner palace.

Shortly after this, an imposing young gentleman in crimson robes made his appearance whom the Dragon King introduced to Liu Yi as Lord Qiantang. Lord Qiantang apologised to Liu Yi for the fright he had given him and praised him for having chivalrously undertaken the service for his niece, who might otherwise have ended her days in the river. He said that in between dealing with his niece's worthless husband and restoring her to her parents he had found time to call on the Celestial Emperor and obtain a pardon for his past misdemeanors but still awaited pardon for the violence which had upset Liu Yi. Liu Yi was charmed by his courtesy.

The King questioned Lord Qiantang about his escapade. Was anyone killed? About 600,000, said Lord Qiantang. No damage to the crops, he hoped. Oh, about 800 square miles. And what about the young husband — what had become of him? I ate him, said Lord Qiantang. Really, said his brother, that was going too far. You mustn't do this kind of thing again.

Next day there was a big feast in Liu Yi's honour in the great hall of the palace attended by all the dragon clan. There was music and dancing, and the Dragon King, Lord Qiantang and Liu Yi all sang songs of their own composition. At the end of the entertainment Liu Yi received many valuable presents from the royal brothers and the other guests.

On the third day there was another party, at which Lord Qiantang became very drunk. He proposed that Liu Yi should marry the now widowed Dragon Princess — an attractive enough proposition, but made in language so crude and threatening that Liu Yi felt bound to refuse. Braving the possible consequences of provoking Lord Qiantang's wrath, he rebuked him for behaving in a manner more suited to his dragon shape than to that of the cultivated young prince which he had assumed. Surprisingly, Lord Qiantang's bluster seemed instantly to deflate and he apologised abjectly for his rudeness.

When at a farewell party next day attended by the Queen and the other ladies of the court the Dragon Princess was called upon to express her thanks to her deliverer, Liu Yi, as he gazed at the vision of loveliness curtseying in front of him and murmuring words of gratitude, began to regret his hasty rejection of Lord Qiantang's offer. More presents were showered on him as he took his leave and a dozen porters were required to carry his accumulated treasure from the lakeside to his home.

Later he travelled with his gifts to Yangchow and had the lot valued in the goldsmiths' quarter of that city. The amount they realised when he sold them meant that overnight he became rich beyond the dreams of avarice. He was able to settle down and take a wife and still have enough to live in luxury for the rest of his life. He married a Miss Zhang, but when they had been married only a few months she took sick and died; and a Miss Han whom he married shortly afterwards also survived for only a few months. Rich but unblessed, Liu Yi moved out east, took a large house in Nanking, and for a time lived on his own in it, a disconsolate widower. Tiring at last of his single estate, he engaged the services of a matchmaker and a marriage was arranged for him with a Miss Lu of Fanyang. She came of a very distinguished family, but her father was dead and her mother, who had remarried, had lately been widowed a second time and was anxious to find a good home for her talented daughter.

Returning home one evening a month or so after his marriage to Miss Lu, Liu Yi was suddenly struck by something about her that reminded him of the Dragon Princess. He told her about his supernatural encounters and remarked on the coincidence of the likeness, but she laughingly dismissed it as his fancy and drove it all from his head by announcing that she was expecting a child. Liu Yi began to feel truly devoted to his new wife.

A month after the birth of the child, which turned out to be a son, his wife put on all her finery and summoned their friends and neighbours to a little party. In the course of it she called her husband to her and asked him if he ever thought about what she must have been like before she was married. Liu Yi had to confess that his thoughts were mainly about the Dragon Princess whom he deeply regretted having rejected. "I *am* the Dragon Princess," said his wife, and went on to explain how she had longed for him after his departure, and how her parents, who had at first wanted to marry her off elsewhere, had finally agreed to let her substitute for the fictitious Miss Lu of Fanyang when it was known that Liu Yi was looking for another wife. She had been very unsure of his real feelings towards her, so she had not dared to admit who she really was until she had given him a son. What had he meant when he expressed a hope, that time when he took leave of her on the banks of the Jing, that she would not refuse to see him if he ever visited her in Lake Dongting?

Liu Yi was obliged to admit that he had not meant to imply any particular feeling for her by that remark. He had felt only sympathy and a desire to help someone in distress. Lord Qiantang's proposal had upset him because it assumed that he would willingly connive at a man's life (in this case a dragon's life) in order to possess his wife, whereas nothing was further from his mind. But he confessed that when they parted and he had some inkling of her feelings for him he had begun to regret his refusal.

After a tearful and highly emotional scene, the Princess assured him that he would now share her immortality and be able to travel in water as well as on land. They paid a visit to her parents in the Dongting Lake and later moved down to Canton where they lived for some years as a human couple, though with no signs of ageing. In the Kai-yuan period (713–742) when the Emperor's growing interest in the supernatural meant that people like Liu Yi and his wife who possessed special knowledge of the supernatural were in danger of recruitment, they deemed it safer to retire permanently, together with their children, to the kingdom beneath the lake, and from then on, except for a couple of appearances to a cousin of Liu Yi's who happened to be travelling in the area, they were never again seen in the world above.

꒞꒞　　　　꒞꒞　　　　꒞꒞　　　　꒞꒞

Liu Yi and The Dragon Princess — A Synopsis

Prelude

Enter Lord Jing, Dragon King of the River Jing, reciting a walking-on quatrain, and introduces himself to the audience. He is concerned about his son's marriage but will wait to hear what he has to say. Enter his son, the Little Dragon, reciting a comic walking-on quatrain. He introduces himself and explains that he detests his wife and hopes to turn his father against her and get rid of her. Brief exchange with his father who is outraged by what he hears and commands Dragon Princess to be summoned. Enter Dragon Princess and announces herself. Lord Jing angrily reproaches her and she kneels to justify herself. Lord Jing orders her to be stripped of her finery and sent to mind sheep on the river-bank. Exeunt all but Dragon Princess, who sings her first two arias. Exit.

Act One

Enter Mother Liu with her son, reciting walking-on quatrain, and introduces herself and her son. When is her son going to reap some reward for all his studies? Examinations begin this spring, says Liu Yi: this is the time, and takes leave of his mother. (Exit Liu Yi.) Now he's gone, says his mother; I shall stay here and wait for the good news. Exit.

Enter Dragon Princess. She introduces herself and describes her predicament, explaining incidentally that the sheep she is minding are not really sheep but off-duty rain-workers, then sings the first three arias of this Act. She says, "When I think of my life in the Dongting Lake and what it's like now, I could die of sorrow." Then she sings the aria "My home's a watery kingdom …".

Enter Liu Yi reciting walking-on quatrain and introduces himself. He has failed in the examinations and is going to visit a friend in Jingyang. This is the bank of the Jing he says. He can see an unusual-looking girl minding sheep who seems very sad. He will ask her what her trouble is. Exchanges greetings with Dragon Princess who tells him of her predicament and asks if he will deliver her letter. "I will," he says, "but shouldn't you try harder to please your husband?" Dragon Princess sings "A single word from me …". Liu Yi then says, "Can you tell me what's so terrible about him?" The Princess sings "When he gets in a rage …". "On the subject of this letter," he asks, "is your home far from here?" She sings "In human terms …". Liu Yi says, "It seems you live under the Dongting Lake. Though I'm willing to take the letter, how could I possibly get there?" The Princess sings an aria explaining the magic pass that will enable him to. "I'll do it then," says Liu Yi and takes the letter. "But will you be willing to see me if I come to visit you afterwards?" "You will be like one of the family," she replies and sings the aria "The reason why …". Exit.

"Was she a spirit or a demon?" Liu Yi asks himself. "At all events, I'll take this letter and see what happens." Exit.

Act Two

Enter Liu Yi and introduces himself. "This is the Dongting Lake and here is the orange-tree she spoke of," he says, and strikes the tree. Enter *yaksha* with walking-on quatrain. Liu Yi introduces himself to the *yaksha* and says he wishes to speak with the Dragon King (Lord Dongting). "Close your eyes and follow me," says the *yaksha*. Exeunt.

Enter Lord Dongting with his Queen and introduces himself. He has been listening to a Taoist lecture but was interrupted by a message to say that someone has been striking the orange-tree. He has ordered the *yaksha* to go and see who it is. Ah, here comes the *yaksha*!

Enter *yaksha* with Liu Yi. "Wait here," he tells Liu Yi, outside an imaginary door, and goes "inside" to announce him. "Bring him in," says Lord Dongting. Liu Yi comes forward and introduces himself. He tells of his meeting with the Princess and delivers the letter. Lord Dongting and his Queen read it. The Queen cries out in grief. "Hush, hush, hush!" says the

King. "Don't let the Fire Dragon hear you." He tells Liu Yi to rest in another room and gives instructions for his entertainment. Exeunt *yaksha* and Liu Yi.

Enter Lord Qiantang (the Fire Dragon) with walking-on quatrain. He introduces himself. "Why do I live here? Because I caused a flood and am condemned to be a prisoner in the cave behind the Qiantang Waterfall. Today is a free day, so I shall go and call on my brother. Ah, here I am!" He tells the *yaksha* to go in and announce him. The *yaksha* announces him and he "enters". After exchanging greetings with Lord Qiantang he remarks on the human smell. "A human scholar has called on important business," says Lord Dongting. "Would you mind leaving us for a few minutes." Lord Qiantang mimes going into another room but listens at the door to overhear what is said. He becomes enraged when he hears his brother and sister-in-law discussing the plight of his niece. "My niece a shepherdess! What a disgrace! I shall mobilise my troops, break my chain (?), fly up to heaven and see the Celestial Emperor about this and deal with the villain." Exit.

Enter *yaksha* and announces to Lord Dongting that the Fire Dragon has gone off with his troops to fight the Little Dragon of the Jing. "This will never do," says Lord Dongting. "We mustn't let our guest know, or he will be frightened. Summon my troops. I shall go to meet my brother." Exit with Queen.

Enter Little Dragon of Jing with troops and introduces himself. "Be ready to meet the Fire Dragon, he is on his way."

Enter Lord Qiantang with troops and commands them to prepare for battle. "Wretch!" he says to the Little Dragon, "I've come to do battle with you!" Simulated fighting ensues. The Little Dragon says, "He's too much for me. Fly! Fly! Fly!" Exit.

Lord Qiantang, "He's clearly no match for me. I shall pursue." Exit.

Enter Little Dragon in haste. "Escape is the best policy. Let me transform myself into a little snake and bury myself in the mud!"

Enter Lord Qiantang. "He ran this way, but where is he?" Catches sight of Little Dragon. "Ah, he's turned himself into a little snake and burrowed into the mud. Don't think you'll escape so easily, my friend! I'll pull him out and swallow him." Does so. "Now I'll go back and report my victory to my brother." Exit.

Enter Lord Jing and introduces himself. "I've sent Mother Lightning to see how the battle went between my son and the Fire Dragon. She should be here by now."

Enter Mother Lightning and sings her first two arias, then she announces that she brings a report of the battle. Lord Jing asks how it went. What follows is a sequence of eight arias, punctuated only by the spoken questions and comments of Lord Jing, in which Mother Lightning narrates the course and outcome of the battle and the circumstances which provoked it. She exits at the end of the eighth aria. Lord Jing then exits after reciting eight lines of verse vowing retaliation for the loss of his son.

Act Three

Enter Lord Dongting with troops.

Enter *yaksha* and reports that Lord Qiantang has returned victorious. Lord Dongting commands his troops to form a welcoming parade.

Enter Lord Qiantang and announces his victory. In an exchange that echoes word for word the one in Li Chaowei's story he asks him about the collateral damage. Lord Dongting then proposes to reward Liu Yi by offering him his daughter in marriage and commands the *yaksha* to ask him in.

Enter Liu Yi. "I have already been waiting here *several days*," he says. "I wonder what they want." Lord Dongting thanks him for saving his daughter and asks if he will consider marrying her. Liu Yi, in an aside, reflects that the shepherdess he met on the banks of the Jing was haggard and ill-favoured. He doesn't want to marry her, and excuses himself on the grounds that it would be improper to marry the widow of a man for whose death he was responsible and also because he has an elderly mother to take care of. This provokes an angry outburst from Lord Qiantang, who apologises, however, in response to Liu Yi's dignified rebuke. Resigned to Liu Yi's rejection of his marriage proposal, Lord Dongting suggests that the Princess should thank him in person and orders the *yaksha* to summon her.

Enter the Dragon Princess and stands outside an imaginary door to the hall. "Just thanking Liu Yi is not going to be enough," she says. Before "entering" the hall, she sings the aria "My scholar-postman …". She sings her second aria "Into the palace hall I go …" while stepping through the imaginary doorway and greeting her parents and Lord Qiantang. Told to greet Liu Yi she sings "With little steps I go …" while doing so. "Who is this lady?" asks Liu Yi. "My daughter," says Lord Dongting. "How different from the shepherdess!" says Liu Yi. "I wish I had known!" "Too late!" says the Dragon Princess, and sings the aria "Though I'm all eagerness …" during which Liu Yi shows signs of becoming amorous. He tells her that he felt obliged to decline the offer of marriage because of his aged mother, to which she replies with the aria "Scholar, it's beyond debate …". Lord Dongting calls for a party in Liu Yi's honour and the Princess sings two arias, "We shan't be tasting …" and "The winds and waters …" while Lord Dongting and Lord Qiantang recite their farewell poems. After ordering the *yaksha* to bring in the dragons' parting presents, she sings "These worthless gifts …" and exits.

Liu Yi bids his farewells and exits.

Lord Dongting and his brother regret the failure of their plan and express a hope that they may find a way of expressing their gratitude to their human benefactor at some future date. Exeunt omnes.

Act Four

Enter Liu Yi's mother. She is still waiting for him to return.

Enter Liu Yi. He says he has just arrived from Lake Dongting and, having failed in the examinations, will have to announce his own arrival. His mother asks him what post he has been awarded. I failed, he says; but I met the Dragon King of Lake Dongting's Third Princess and carried a letter for her to his palace under the lake where I was given rich presents. Never mind about all that, says his mother, I have arranged a marriage for you and today is the day when your bride will arrive here. Liu Yi protests that, though he refused the hand of the Dragon Princess in marriage, he cannot help thinking about her, but his mother tells him that he must forget the Princess and do as he is told.

Enter the Dragon Princess with the Matchmaker. She introduces herself and explains that her parents have allowed her to impersonate the Miss Lu of Fanyang whom Liu Yi is to marry. She sings her first aria "In a double lotus-plant …". Sound of wedding-music. "What's that?" asks the Princess. "Wedding music," says the Matchmaker. The Princess sings "Bright wedding-lights …". The Matchmaker now takes over and conducts the marriage ceremony. Liu Yi remarks on the likeness of the new bride to the Dragon Princess and questions the Matchmaker about her. The Princess sings "He seems most anxious to know everything …". "Don't you remember me?" she asks Liu Yi. "How could I," says Liu Yi, "we've never met before." The

Princess sings "When I was a lonely slave …" and "Don't you remember …". "Amazing!" says Liu Yi, and tells his mother that this Miss Lu is in fact the Third Princess. The Princess sings "You were my saviour …" and "Come then! …" while she mimes conducting Liu Yi and his mother over an imaginary bridge leading into the supernatural world and ending in the Dragon King's palace beneath Lake Dongting.

Enter Lord Dongting with his Queen, leading a welcoming band of musicians. He greets the newcomers. "Who would have thought I should live to see this day!" Liu Yi exclaims. The Princess sings her final aria "Rescued in rags …" and Lord Dongting steps forward to address the audience and recites the epilogue.

In Li Chaowei's story months or even years elapse between Liu Yi's leaving Lake Dongting with his presents and his marriage to the pseudo Miss Lu of Fanyang. In the course of this time he becomes a rich man, is twice married, and lives for a period as a disconsolate widower. After his marriage to the Princess more years elapse before they and their children disappear into the kingdom beneath the lake. Clearly, the first problem that faces anyone attempting a dramatisation of Li's story is how to deal with the passage of time.

Shang Zhongxian's solution is to abolish it altogether. He does this by inventing the character of Liu Yi's widowed mother. The existence of a widowed mother is referred to once in Li Chaowei's story as one of the reasons given by Liu Yi for his rejection of Lord Dongting's offer of his daughter's hand in marriage, but apart from that there is no mention of her at all. In Shang's *zaju*, on the other hand, although she is not given much to say, she is quite an important character. When Liu Yi gets home from the lake she shows little interest in his adventure with the dragons and the rich presents he has brought with him. It seems that *she* has arranged (presumably during his absence) his marriage with the spurious Miss Lu. In this way Shang is able to cut out the story of Liu Yi's enrichment and of his two previous marriages. The revelation that Miss Lu is really the Third Princess now takes place within a few minutes of her marriage to Liu Yi, and the transformation scene in which she conveys Liu Yi and his mother to the Dragon King's palace in the lake takes place only a few minutes later. The years between Liu Yi's return home from the palace beneath the lake and his permanent retirement to it with the Dragon Princess are concertinaed into a single day.

The other major problem that faced Shang in his dramatisation was the appearance of Lord Qiantang in dragon shape, which is so important a feature of Li Chaowei's story. In Li's story the lamentations of the womenfolk alert Lord Qiantang to his niece's fate and he breaks out of his captivity to rescue her *as a dragon*, thereby half frightening Liu Yi to death. This is the only part of the story in which a dragon's appearance is essential. Qiantang's aerial battle with the River Dragon and his other activities in dragon shape are not described in Li's story, which merely has Qiantang referring to them when he reports back to his brother in human shape.

Shang's solution is to avoid the necessity of showing a dragon on stage by narrating *all* Qiantang's actions in dragon shape in the lyrics sung by the *dan* in Act Two. Most of them are about the battle, but one of them entitled *Sheng yao wang* describes Qiantang's breaking out of captivity:

> *When the Queen heard its message, she was so distressed*
> *That the sound of her weeping reached Qiantang in his cage.*
> *The great gold chain that bound him was broken in his rage.*
> *Like a twig he snapped it and, in his dragon shape,*
> *High into the sky above he made his escape.*

In the Ming text of the *zaju* that has come down to us Act Two reads not like one act but two. There is the version in the second half of the act in which the *dan* in the character of Mother Lightning sings eleven lyrics narrating, in somewhat jumbled order, all the action from the arrival of Liu Yi at the lakeside to the defeat of the River Dragon and his attempt to escape Qiantang's vengeance by burrowing into the mud; but before that there is the first half of the act, involving most of the other actors and consisting entirely of spoken dialogue, in which the entire action from Liu Yi's arrival at the lakeside to Lord Qiantang's swallowing of the little snake is shown in quite a different version. In the lyrics sung by the *dan* in the second half of the act the battle between the dragons is described as an epic struggle of almost cosmic proportions:

> *The dragons pluck islands out of the sea*
> *And threaten to topple the sacred hills*

or, in another lyric:

> *When they hurled themselves forward to attack*
> *The whole world seemed to tremble and reel back.*

It's almost impossible to believe that the clownish scamperings in the spoken first half of the act could have been conceived by the author of these lyrics in the second half. I strongly suspect that the spoken first half of Act Two up to the entry of the *dan* was the work of the actors themselves and that the second half, from the entry of the *dan* onwards, was the original Act Two supplied to them by Shang Zhongxian. The actors probably thought that Shang's static, cantata-like solution would be above the heads of their audience and decided to supply a more dynamic version of their own to precede it. The difficulty of doing so with their limited resources is apparent.

One of the limitations was that of number — the small number of players available in an average-sized company. You can see this from the fact that in the Dragon King's realm the only subordinate given a part is the overworked *yaksha*, who appears to be lakeside patrol, messenger, doorman, butler and general factotum. The part of the Matchmaker in the last act may have been taken by the same player. As for the stage armies, they were probably half-a-dozen musicians doubling as extras. (They do in fact appear on the stage at the end of the play as a welcoming band.) The biggest limitation of all, however, was the impossibility of representing a really convincing dragon on the stage. The attempt to dodge the necessity of showing one had a bizarre effect on the plot.

Because Liu Yi couldn't be shown on the stage being frightened by the sight of Lord Qiantang in his dragon shape, he has to be shunted offstage as soon as the Dragon King has read the letter. The Queen, always present with the Dragon King in this *zaju*, cries out in grief when she reads it and has to be silenced; but this echo of Li's story has lost its point, because Lord Qiantang has not yet arrived on the premises. When shortly afterwards he ambles in on a visit to his brother, some other means than the Queen's anguished cries must be found of alerting him to his niece's plight and provoking his homicidal rage; so he, too, must be shunted out of the way, not offstage this time but into an imaginary "other room" where he can overhear his brother and sister-in-law discussing the letter. Then, in an angry soliloquy addressed to the audience, he states his intention of mobilising his troops and going off to deal with the obnoxious husband and vindicate the family honour. A slightly comical interlude ensues in which he and the young River Dragon confront themselves with their stage "armies" and engage in what Shakespeare calls "alarms and excursions". It concludes with a scene in which the victorious Lord Qiantang consumes, for the audience's delectation no doubt, the tiny snake into which the young River Dragon is believed to have transformed himself.

One consequence of all these changes is that when Liu Yi re-appears on stage in Act Three he has not previously seen Lord Qiantang in any shape. Nor has he seen the Dragon Princess since he met her as a shepherdess on the banks of the Jing. When offered the Princess's hand in marriage by her father, he gives his obligation to care for his widowed mother as an excuse for declining, but confesses in an aside that the real reason he doesn't want to marry her is because when he met her as a shepherdess she looked so unattractive. Later he regrets his refusal when told that the beautiful young woman just summoned to the party is in fact the same person.

This is quite different from Li Chaowei's story in which the Princess, when he first met her as a shepherdess, struck Liu Yi as beautiful even though she looked ill and unhappy. In Li's story he next sees her passing into the inner apartments of the palace when she gets back to Lake Dongting and is able to identify her as the same beautiful young woman he had met on the banks of the Jing. In the story it's the uncle, not the Dragon King, who first proposes that Liu Yi should marry her, and Liu Yi rejects the offer not because he had found her unattractive but because of the insulting way in which the offer was made.

As in Act Two, these instances where the action of the *zaju* differs from the plot of the original story occur in a long section of spoken dialogue which comes before the entry of the *dan*; and since there is nothing in the lyrics to suggest the need for such changes, it's tempting to conclude that they are an invention of the actors rather than the work of Shang Zhongxian himself.

Some elements of Li's story which are preserved in the spoken dialogue seem superfluous or incongruous in their new context, like Lord Qiantang's colourful threat that Liu Yi will be "down in the shit" if he doesn't marry the Princess. The story gives this as the reason for Liu Yi's rejection of the marriage-offer, but in the *zaju* it is superfluous because the offer has already been made by the Dragon King and he has already rejected it. Another example is the Princess's explanation that the sheep she is minding are not really sheep but "rain-workers". In the story it is the answer she gives when Liu Yi asks why spirits who don't eat mutton should want to keep sheep, but in the *zaju* she rather incongruously gives this information while she is introducing herself to the audience and just before launching into a pathetic aria about the sadness of her fate. No doubt there was a section of the audience who would want to hear these well-known features of the story repeated in the *zaju*, just as children hearing a familiar fairy-tale will insist, however much other parts of the story may vary in the telling, that the giant in Jack and Beanstalk should always say "Fee, fie, foh, fum" and the grandmother in Little Red Riding Hood should invariably tell Riding Hood to "Lift up the latch, open the door, and walk in!" I strongly suspect that these rather clumsy attempts at incorporating familiar elements into the play were, like the changes mentioned above, the work of the actors rather than of Shang Zhongxian himself.

Yet whether the actors were responsible for all the dialogue or only for alterations in it, the lyrics in this, as in all *zaju*, were by far the most important part. Ironically the first Chinese drama to be introduced to the West was a *zaju* from which all the lyrics had been omitted. In his *Petit orphelin de la famille Tchao*, published in 1735 as part of Du Halde's encyclopœdic collection of Jesuit writings on China, Prémare gives only the spoken dialogue of the *zaju*, openly confessing that he found translating the lyrics too difficult. When he comes to a lyric, he simply writes *"Il chante"* and leaves it out — a curious reversal of the practice observed in early Chinese editions of giving only the lyrics and printing "He speaks" when they come to some dialogue. Père Prémare's translation inspired Voltaire to write a sub-Racinian tragedy in verse called *L'orphelin de la Chine* which was staged with some success in 1755. It was not remotely like anything Chinese.

Other translations of *zaju* which do include the lyrics have been made in various European languages during the two and a half centuries since Prémare's day but I don't think any have been staged, certainly not with musical accompaniment. Translations of *zaju* aren't much fun to read, for the same reason, I suppose, that translations of the libretti of European operas aren't much fun to read unless you have heard them sung and want to find out what the words are.

Having decided to make an adaptation of this *zaju* that could be staged, it seemed to me that the first step must be to try and produce a singable version of the lyrics that could be set to music. My translation of them is very free, as any rhymed translation of Chinese verse is bound to be, and probably contains a fair number of inaccuracies. All I can say is that I have translated all of them and that they are in their original order.

When it came to the spoken parts of the *zaju*, I decided in the end to abandon the Chinese text altogether and make up my own. I did this for several reasons. First of all, by abandoning the Chinese practice of making the characters introduce themselves and substituting a Narrator I was able to explain things that the original Chinese audience would have known without needing to be told but which a Western audience might not understand.

Secondly I wanted to remove as far as possible the inconsistencies between what is said or implied in the lyrics and what is said or implied in the Chinese dialogue. This involved major alterations in the action of the play which had the effect of making it conform more closely to the original story.

The original story by Li Chaowei is, in its way, quite a subversive one. The conventional hero in Chinese stories is a poor scholar who marries the Prime Minister's daughter and becomes rich and famous after devoting all his formative years to study and passing out top in the Imperial examinations. By contrast Liu Yi, in spite of being a total flop in his exams, becomes unimaginably rich, marries a fairy princess and wins immortality. The ideal young woman would never take the initiative in her dealings (if she had any) with the opposite sex, would unquestioningly marry the husband of her parents' choice, and would under no circumstances remarry if she became a widow. The Dragon Princess pursues the man of her choice with single-minded determination and she contemplates remarriage without a moment's hesitation, but is dismissive of her parents' choice of a second husband.

Modern Chinese scholars sometimes point to the Third Princess as a prototype of the liberated woman who believes in expressing herself freely and marrying the man of her choice; but I suspect she belongs more to the category of wish-fulfilment fantasy. The young men who came up to the capital to take the Imperial examinations, on their own in a big city perhaps for the first time in their lives, dreamed of a degree of sexual freedom which they were usually without the experience, confidence or means to attain. Ideally beautiful and talented young women able and willing to make themselves available existed only in their imaginations: they would have to be either well-born young ladies with an unheard-of freedom of movement, expensive prostitutes prepared to offer their services gratis, or supernatural beings like fox-fairies or dragon princesses — the heroines, in short, of the class of Tang stories to which Li Chaowei's *Liu Yi zhuan* belongs.

In taking over this story for his *zaju* Shang makes much of the Princess's sense of obligation. Non-humans like dragons, he says, have as much sense of honour as men. The Princess was motivated by an overwhelming desire to repay Liu Yi's kindness and good faith. But there is more than a hint that her feeling for him was rather more than gratitude and that she had set her heart on marrying him from the start. Just what we are meant to make of Liu Yi is less clear. It's quite obvious, as it is in Li Chaowei's story, that he didn't entirely reciprocate the feelings of the Princess, as she herself could see. She thinks he is inhibited by his conventional attitudes. A bit "stuffy", we should say. If we accept that view of him, which seems quite compatible both with what we are told about him in Li's story and what we can gather from the lyrics, he becomes quite an interesting character; whereas if we follow the text of the spoken dialogue that I have rejected, which has him turning down the Dragon King's offer on the grounds of her looks, it makes him seem merely contemptible.

I am aware that my rewriting of the spoken parts of this *zaju* depends on a highly subjective interpretation, but what I have written is an adaptation, not a reconstruction aimed at an "authentic" production. (If such a thing were possible, it would be much better left to Chinese experts.) This is a version for an English language production, made for the entertainment of an English-speaking audience. How it is produced will depend very much on the producer and the resources available. I hope it can be fairly spectacular; but however it is done, as long as the lyrics sound good, the audience will get at least *some* idea of a Yuan *zaju*, which up to now has been scarcely possible.

Liu Yi and the Dragon Princess

Prologue

XIAN LÜ

[*The Narrator appears in mid-stage. He is bare-headed and clothed from head to foot in a single plain black garment.*]

NARRATOR: Fu Xi, the great civiliser, who invented the Eight Mystic Trigrams and taught men how to hunt and fish and how to keep flocks and herds, had trusty ministers to help him in his work. These men, when their human lives had ended, were transformed by the Celestial Emperor into dragons. They became the Dragon Kings who live in the depths of lakes and rivers and control the clouds and rain. When they are about their business, flying through the air, wreathed in storm-clouds and with lightnings flashing about them, they can be very terrible; but at other times they can appear in human shape and look just like us.

Here, in his human shape, is the Dragon King of the Jing, a river in north-west China.

[*A tall figure appears on his left, dressed in dragon robes and with a dragon crown on his head.*]

Lord Jing is worried about his son, the Young Lord, who recently married the third daughter of the Dragon King of Lake Dongting in the distant South.

[*A second figure, dressed somewhat like the first, appears on his right.*]

The son is a young libertine, debauched by his servant-girls and pages. He hates his new wife and maltreats her; but Lord Jing is an indulgent father and unlikely to blame him for the breakdown of their marriage. As you will see, the Young Lord is hoping to play on his father's weakness to rid himself of his unwanted wife.

[*The Narrator disappears. There are now seen to be several other figures in the background.*]

LORD JING: My son and this Third Princess from Lake Dongting don't seem to get on together. I'm very unhappy about this marriage; but I'd better wait to see what my boy has got to say about it.

YOUNG LORD: Father, this dragon-girl you chose for me is a thoroughly bad lot. We've been at cross purposes ever since she came here. She uses her father's importance as an excuse for throwing her weight about and getting the better of me. I don't think even you count for much in her estimation.

LORD JING: This is preposterous! Call the wretched creature here at once somebody! I know how to deal with *her*.

[*Sound of assenting "Hai!" from one of background figures who hurries offstage to fetch her. Enter the Dragon Princess. She too is magnificently dressed, like the other two. She curtseys to Lord Jing and glances apprehensively towards her husband.*]

DRAGON PRINCESS: You asked to see me, father-in-law. What is it you want?

LORD JING: [*Angrily*] What do you mean by this unacceptable behaviour I have been hearing about? Why can't you behave like a proper wife? You'd better change your ways pretty quickly, or you'll have *me* to deal with and you'll find you won't get away with it quite so easily.

DRAGON PRINCESS: [*Kneeling*] But father-in-law, I've done nothing at all to upset my husband. It's because he listens to what his maids tell him. They make all sorts of trouble between us. A daughter of Dragon Kings can't be expected to submit to shrimps and fishes.

LORD JING: Pshaw! Look at her! She defies even *me* now! I'm not surprised that my poor dragon-boy finds her so difficult. Guards, strip off her crown and robes! Let her keep sheep for us beside the river.

[*Two of the attendant figures come forward, drag the Princess roughly to her feet and proceed to take off her crown, her robes and all her jewellery. Meantime Lord Jing recites the following.*]

    A few years tending sheep here in disgrace
    Should teach this shrewish wife her proper place.
    But all the Jing's waters will not wash away
    The shameful blot that marks her from this day.

[*While he is reciting this, the figures on the stage all gradually disappear. After a brief pause, the figure of the Dragon Princess appears on the centre of the stage, but now completely transformed: her hair is tousled, her face is pale and drawn and she is dressed in rags.*]

DRAGON PRINCESS: [*Sings*]

Duan zheng hao

Now all my springtime years are to be wasted:
The married joys they told me of untasted.
Now I'm to be abandoned and alone,
A dried-up lake from which the birds have flown.
I could not bear my husband's cruel spite;
His parents, too — for whom
I could do nothing right.

Yao pian

So now they're rid of me: a shepherdess!
His little plan has been a great success.
Hard hearts like theirs will know no alteration:
Here I must stay, amidst this desolation,
For palace, a deserted fishing station;
My hair like a haystack,
My face in a frown,
Constantly grieving,
My tears running down.
And my parents, my dear ones — ah, Heaven above!
Shall I ever again see the ones that I love?

Act One

[*The Narrator appears with two other figures, one on each side of him, one of them seated, the other standing. After introducing them he disappears.*]

NARRATOR: Here are Liu Yi and his mother. They live in a town called Xiangyin* on the east bank of the River Xiang, very near Lake Dongting where the Dragon Princess's family live. Liu Yi is a scholar, already twenty-three years old but still unmarried. His mother is a widow and they are very poor, so he cannot afford to marry, though his mother would like to have a grandson and he owes it to his dead father to carry on the family name. The Triennial Examinations are to be held this year in the Imperial Capital and Liu Yi thinks he may have a chance of succeeding in them and winning a place for himself in the bureaucracy.

LIU YI: Mother, it's the Spring Examination in the Capital this year, I've seen the proclamation. After studying so hard all these years, I've got quite a lot under my belt. I think I should stand a chance. It would be an honour for the whole family if I succeeded. I'd be a great man — well, an official of some kind or other! What do you think, Mother?

---

* The Chinese text of the *zaju* gives "Huaiyin" as the place where Liu Yi and his mother lived, but this is almost certainly an error for *Xiangyin*. Li Chaowei's story says that Liu Yi's home town was *Xiangbin* ("on the bank of the R. Xiang"). Xiangyin is on the east bank of the R. Xiang not far from Lake Dongting. Huaiyin is in Jiangsu 450 miles away.

MRS LIU: That's what all this studying is for, isn't it, my son? I'm sure you could succeed if you set your mind to it.

LIU YI: Today's a lucky day for travelling: I've looked in the calendar. I'd like to start straight away.

MRS LIU: Go then, my boy, and your mother's blessing go with you! I shall stay here at home and wait for the good news.

[*The scene changes to reveal the Dragon Princess as she was at the end of the Prologue, except that now she is surrounded with grazing sheep, each moving forward a few steps from time to time to choose a new patch of grass.*]

DRAGON PRINCESS:

[*She sings*]   *Dian jiang chun*

    Dejected, anguished, often weeping,

    I try to dream the way back when I'm sleeping.

    Now spring has ended, shall I ever make

    While I'm awake

    That journey to my home beneath the lake,

    And tell them in one long narration,

    All I have suffered since our separation?

      Hun jiang long

    There were pretty maids to wait on me back there

    Dressing with crystal combs my piled-up hair;

    But now my clothes are ragged and threadbare,

    My haggard face is lined with care.

    No fairy prince sought me in marriage,

    A flying phoenix for his carriage;

    Though I'm a spirit, I'm condemned for ever

    To be a shepherd-slave beside this river.

    I think of our

    First days together

    When I tried hard

    To give him pleasure:

Clawing and clutching me,
Down on me bearing,
He was so violent and so uncaring:
When I protested
He would shout:
How could things ever
Have worked out?
Better endure this solitary life
Than live in luxury with all that strife.

When I think of those days before my marriage, that easy life in my home beneath the lake — I was so happy then — and so comfortable. But look at me now!

[*She sings*]   *You hu lu*
I'm grimed with the dust and sand that blow
                                        here everywhere.
My looks are past repair:
Only my tears and the rain to wash my face,
And the wind to comb my hair.
Often, like Su Wu on the frozen plain,
I find myself gazing homewards, though I know
I gaze in vain.
I find no comfort, whether I sit or lie,
And when I walk, at every step I sigh.

[*She extracts a letter from her ragged clothing and examines it carefully.*]
I've written a letter to my parents, but how am I going to send it? It's little likely that anyone will ever come this way, or that they would be willing and able to carry it for me so far even if they did.

[*She sings*]   *Tian xia le*
My home's a watery kingdom under a southern
                                        sky.
I've written to them, but can't send the letter:

For wintering geese it's much too far to fly;
The faithful hound has not the strength to try;
And stupid fish would never find the way.
I can only wait and pray
Communications will get better.

[*The scene fades and the Narrator appears.*]

NARRATOR: Liu Yi's hopes were dashed. He didn't get a place in
the Spring Examination and now he must return, an ignominious
failure, to his home in the south. A fellow-townsman he knows of
has a post in Jingyang, a town on the Jing River not too far from
the Capital. He thought he would make a detour to visit him and
has just left after spending a few days as his guest. Now he is making his way along the river bank. Mysteriously the horse he is travelling
on has just taken fright. After mastering it, he sees this solitary girl
ahead apparently tending a flock of sheep. He notices that there is
something rather striking about her, despite her rags and her sallow and
grimy features. He also notices that she appears to be very much
distressed. He dismounts and walks ahead to meet her.

[*The Narrator disappears and we are back again with the Dragon
Princess and her sheep. Enter Liu Yi, he has a cloth bag rather like a satchel
over one of his shoulders. He advances to the Dragon Princess, clasps his
hands and bows.*]

LIU YI: Your servant, young lady.

DRAGON PRINCESS: [*Curtseying*] Your servant, sir. May I ask
who you are and where you are from, and what it is that brings you
here?

LIU YI: My name is Liu Yi and I come from Xiangyin.* I've failed in
the examination and I just happen to be passing this way on my
journey home. May I ask who *you* are, young lady, and how you come
to be minding sheep in this unlikely place?

---

* See footnote on p. 35.

DRAGON PRINCESS: I am called the Third Princess, the daughter of a Dragon King. My father married me to the son of the Dragon King of the Jing River. My husband is cruel and violent and his servant-girls are always making trouble between us. My father-in-law thinks it's all my fault and has sent me to mind sheep here on this river-bank as a punishment. I have to get up at dawn every day and don't finish until it's dark, and I'm exposed to the weather all day long. That's why I look so awful. [*She pauses a moment before going on.*] There's something I want to ask you. I've written a letter to my family telling them about this, but so far I haven't found any means of sending it. Now that chance has brought you my way, I'd like to ask you if *you* could deliver it to my father for me, but I don't know whether you'd be willing to or not.

LIU YI: I've always been taught that you should help people when they are in trouble; and after what you've told me, of course I'd be willing. But wouldn't it have been better if you'd been a bit more yielding in the first place? You might have saved yourself this hardship?

DRAGON PRINCESS: You don't know what I had to put up with. [*She sings*]   *Na zha ling*

> A single word from me would
> Provoke a ton of trouble —
> Provoke a ton of trouble,
> And trouble would redouble
> My sorrow and my longing
> To be back home again.
> My marriage brought no comfort,
> But suffering and pain.
> We were an ill-matched couple from the start,
> But his uncertain temper
> First drove us apart.

LIU YI: You say he has an uncertain temper. What exactly do you mean by that? Can you describe it to me?

DRAGON PRINCESS:
[*She sings*]   *Que ta zhi*

> When he gets in a rage, you can see his chest
>   inflate.
> When he's scowling with hate, his whiskers stand
>   up straight.
> When he opens his mouth, what come out are
>   not pearls,
> But from his jaws a foggy cloud unfurls.
> His cough makes a wind and a sharp squall of rain,
> Sucked up from the earth to fall on earth again.

LIU YI: Well, I'll deliver your letter for you if I can. But where is your home, and how far away is it from here?

DRAGON PRINCESS:
[*She sings*]   *Ji sheng cao*

> In human terms, five hundred leagues of space
> Divide my home from this unfriendly place.
> Far over the white duckweed and the haze,
> Beneath the cold waters, shrouded from men's gaze.

LIU YI: Your home is in a lake, then? You say you are a princess. I suppose you must live in a palace. What do they call the place where you live? Phoenix Hall?

DRAGON PRINCESS: [*Sings*]

> Where I was born there was no Phoenix Hall.
> There *was* a Parrot Island, I recall.

LIU YI: Ah, now I understand. Your home is in the Dongting Lake. But Princess, if you're really a dragon princess, you must be some sort of spirit. I'm only a human being. How on earth do I get to the bottom of Lake Dongting to deliver your letter?

DRAGON PRINCESS: [*She fishes the letter from her rags again and hands it to him.*] Now that you have agreed to deliver the letter, I will tell you how to get to my father's palace. [*She hands him a large golden hairpin, the size of a fairly big tent-peg.*] As you approach the lake you will see a little temple. In front of the temple there is an altar with an orange-tree growing beside it. The village folk think of this orange-tree as their protector and make offerings to it. Strike the tree with this golden hairpin and a guardian will appear who will take you where want to go to.

[*She sings*]   *Yao pian*

There is an altar on the golden strand
Beside which grows a golden orange-tree.
This golden pin you must hold in your hand
And strike the tree with it. Then you will see
Rise from the water, leaving a golden track,
A spirit who will take you on his back
And swiftly and safely, through a watery passage,
Bear you to those who will receive your message.

LIU YI: I'll be your postman, then, and deliver this letter for you. I hope that some time in the future, if you ever get back to your Dongting palace, you won't try to avoid seeing me if I come to visit you.

DRAGON PRINCESS: If you deliver this letter for me, you will be my saviour. Not only shall I *not* avoid seeing you, I shall treat you as one of my own family.

[*She sings*]   *Zhuan sha*

The reason why
I shun to go where love-birds fly,
Or contemplate
The mandarin ducks, each with a loving mate:
It is because I think of my own fate,
Wedded to one so full of rage and hate.
But though I lived with him beneath the river,
No fish of his came in my waters ever.
So do not hesitate,

If you should wish to change your single state.
Look at my grateful tears, as thick as dew!
If I escape from here to something better,
Kind-hearted gentleman, it will be thanks to you:
For all my hopes lie in this tear-stained letter.

[*She vanishes.*]

LIU YI: I wonder who or what she really is. Whatever she is, here are the hairpin and the letter. I'd better find that temple on the shore of Lake Dongting and see what happens.

Act Two

YÜE DIAO

NARRATOR: After weeks of travel Liu Yi has reached the shores of Lake Dongting and found the temple. Everything is exactly as the Dragon Princess had said. *There* is the altar, and *there* beside it is the great orange-tree, laden with golden fruit. He taps the bark of the tree with the golden hairpin that the Princess has given him and waits. Presently a head emerges from the waters of the lake, gazes at him inquiringly, and is followed after a few moments by the rest of the body of a very strange creature, a *yaksha*, who asks him who he is and what he wants. He says that he is Liu Yi and that he has a message for Lord Dongting, the Dragon King of the lake. The *yaksha* tells him to get on his back, hold on tightly, and close his eyes. Liu Yi becomes aware that he is moving rapidly and he has a rushing noise in his ears, but no sensation of being in the water. We shall, however, arrive in the Dragon Hall of the palace before he does.

[*The Narrator disappears. We are in the hall of the Dragon King. It is a bit like a large underwater cavern in a coral reef. There is a subaqueous look about the light, but it is by no means gloomy. Fish are seen swimming outside the large windows. The courtiers, who are themselves all crustaceans or fishes of one kind or other, are waiting for the arrival of the Dragon King (Lord Dongting) and his Queen, around whose empty throne they are grouped. Enter the Dragon King and Queen, chatting, and seat themselves on the throne.*]

QUEEN: I was rather enjoying that lecture. Those Taoist philosophers are so interesting. I like the stories they tell. Why did you make him break off so suddenly?

LORD DONGTING: I was enjoying the lecture, too. The reason I made him break it off is because I had just received a report that a man has been tapping on our orange-tree. I sent the *yaksha* to see who he was and bring him here. In fact, he ought to have arrived by now. [*Enter Liu Yi.*] Ah, here he is! A scholar, it seems.

[*He rises and steps forward to meet his guest. Liu Yi clasps his hands and bows low in greeting. Lord Dongting returns the salutation, graciously but not deferentially.*]

LORD DONGTING: Living out of the way here at the bottom of this lake I am not very well informed about what goes on above. I have to confess that I do not know who you are, sir. It is good of you to have undertaken what must have been a hazardous journey to get here. Have you perhaps some teaching to impart?

LIU YI: My name is Liu Yi and my home is in Xiangyin.* I have been to the Capital to sit for the Spring Examination. I failed. On my way back home I happened to be travelling along the bank of the River Jing when I met a young lady in charge of a flock of sheep who turned out to be your Third Princess. She seemed very unhappy. She was very thin and — well, she didn't look at all like a princess. She asked me to deliver this letter. It is addressed to you.

[*He takes the letter from his satchel, bows, and presents it with both hands to Lord Dongting, who reads it with signs of astonishment and grief.*]

LORD DONGTING: Is it possible! [*He hands the letter to the Queen.*] I blame myself for this. I should have listened to the voices of those who opposed this match. I should never have married the poor child so far from home.

[*The Queen, who has been reading the letter, gives a cry, which she unsuccessfully attempts to stifle.*]

THE QUEEN: Oh, my child! my poor child!

LORD DONGTING: You had better take this letter inside and read it to the others. Only do be careful that Lord Qiantang doesn't get to hear of this. [*Exit Queen. Lord Dongting's grief suddenly gets the better of*

---

* See footnote on p. 35.

him. He covers his face with his sleeve and sobs, but soon recovers himself.]
Forgive me — a momentary weakness. My dear young man, we are all
inexpressibly grateful to you for this service. To think that you, a total
stranger, should take pity on my poor daughter when her own family
had failed her! We didn't hear from her, you see, and we took her
silence for a good sign. But you are an important guest and I am
neglecting you. [*He waves him to a seat.*] Do make yourself comfortable!
[*To an attendant*] Bring some refreshment for Mr Liu. He needs
something to restore him after his long journey.

LIU YI: May I venture to ask, sir, who is this Lord Qiantang, and
why is it so important that he shouldn't hear about your daughter?

LORD DONGTING: Lord Qiantang is my younger brother, the
Dragon King of the Qiantang River. He is by nature extremely violent
and impetuous and has, over the centuries, been responsible for a
number of natural disasters. Because of the last major flood he caused,
the Celestial Emperor sentenced him to long-term imprisonment but
commuted his sentence to confinement on these premises in return for
services I had rendered in the past. We are obliged to keep him on a
chain, however, and are responsible for anything he might do if we let
him out.

[*A sound of lamentation is heard from off-stage.*]
For goodness sake! Lord Qiantang is bound to hear that. [*To an
attendant*] Do tell them to make less noise.

[*The attendant hurries off. There is a moment of complete silence while
Lord Dongting and Liu Yi follow the attendant with their eyes. Then
suddenly there is a tremendous crash, a red flash and a cloud of smoke, and
a huge red dragon flies upwards from the wings, trailing a golden chain
behind him with a broken-off section of pillar attached to it. Liu Yi has
already flung himself to the ground.*]

LORD DONGTING: Too late.

[*He notices that Liu Yi still lies prone upon the ground, raises him up
with the help of an attendant and seats him on a chair. Liu Yi sits there in
shock with his mouth wide open and for a time is visibly shaking.*]

LIU YI: [*Finding his voice at last*] Is it safe for me to go now?

LORD DONGTING: My dear young man, you mustn't dream of going yet. In the first place, we have to reward you as best we can for your service. In the second place, I don't doubt that Lord Qiantang has gone to get my daughter back, and I am sure she will want to thank you in person when she returns. My brother, if you see him again, is unlikely to appear to you in dragon shape and, except when he is angry, he can be perfectly amiable. And I'm pretty sure that, under the circumstances, the Celestial Emperor will overlook any little damage that might occur while he is rescuing her, since in this case it is so clearly that detestable young husband of hers who is the guilty party. Let me show you to a more comfortable apartment where you can relax and recover from your unpleasant shock while I try to discover exactly what my impetuous young brother has been up to.

[*The scene fades and we see the Narrator again.*]

NARRATOR: Lord Dongting's impetuous younger brother, after breaking out of his prison in the form of a fire-dragon, first disposed of the chain and the fragment of pillar that encumbered him and then, gathering together a small army of water-spirits, flew off in a northwesterly direction to deal with his niece's recreant husband. What chiefly outraged him was what he considered the reproach to his own and his family's honour occasioned by his niece's menial employment as a shepherdess. Only when the husband was punished and his honour was vindicated would he consider restoring her to her anxious parents. The outcome of his struggle with the Young Lord was foreseeable. The course of it is described in some detail to the Young Lord's father, the old Dragon King of the River Jing, by a spirit called Mother Lightning, whom the old Jing dragon had employed as an observer. Mother Lightning makes the lightning-flash by means of two metal reflectors which she holds, one in each hand. She and the Thunder God make a team; but on this occasion the Thunder God seems to have been employed elsewhere.

[*The Narrator disappears. Enter Mother Lightning, breathless and staggering a little as if she has just landed on her feet from a great height.*

During most of the scene which follows, while Mother Lightning is singing there is some sort of representation going on in the background of the action she is describing.]

MOTHER LIGHTNING:
[*She sings*]   *Dou an chun*
> The two dragons fought across the sky
> Now east, now west, now low, now high,
> Hidden in cloud or glimpsed through gaps,
> Then down where the water heaves and laps:
> Through a dense cloud of smoke they sped,
> That with breathed-out flames glowed fiery red;
> Flash upon flash the lightning darted
> Each time the smoke of battle parted;
> Shrieking and freaking the weird wind howled
> While the rumbling thunder crashed and growled.

>   *Zi hua er xu*
> Home-going woodcutters nearly died of fright;
> Herb-gatherers panicked at the sight;
> Fishermen at their nets fainted outright.
> Where beds of river-lotuses had been,
> Crimson amidst the canopy of green,
> Now nothing could be seen
> But ranks of warriors mustering for the fight.

Lord Jing, Lord Jing! [*Enter Lord Jing. She continues singing while she is waiting for him to come.*]

> I nearly lost my footing in the air,
> Fell to the earth and damaged these precious things
> Beyond repair.

LORD JING: You must have had a good view of everything from your place up there in the clouds. Tell me, Mother Lightning, how did it go? Take your time. I want to hear it all, from the beginning.

MOTHER LIGHTNING:

[*She sings*]   *Xiao tao hong*

    In his river palace the Young Lord was holding a
                         great feast.
    There was drinking from gold cups to the music's
                      merry sound
    No one saw that far off a black cloud had been
                      gathering,
    That wrapped them all suddenly in darkness profound.
    Then high overhead came a dreadful clap of thunder,
    A wind ripped off the roof-tiles and scattered them
                      around;
    Rafters and roof-brackets sailed through the air,
    And with myriad tinklings the crystal walls
    Came crashing to the ground.

LORD JING: That fiery Qiantang is a fierce, reckless fellow; but I'm sure my boy could give as good as he got. Fire against water. Wind and rain. There would be a great boiling up of rivers, a great shaking and quaking of the earth. Tell me just how it was, Mother Lightning. Tell me how the fiery Qiantang raged and how my brave boy resisted.

MOTHER LIGHTNING:

[*She sings*]   *Zi hua er xu*

    Quick as a flash
    Together clash
    The sky above with the earth below,
    Dark clouds lowering,
    Waters towering,
    And lightnings darting to and fro.
    Up from the river the Young Lord flies,
    Qiantang pursuing him into the skies;
    There the two dragons prepared to fight,
    And Colonel Sturgeon and Captain Turtle,
    Gazing up at the fearsome sight,

Were all but paralysed with fright.
Displaying their supernatural skills,
The dragons pluck islands out of the sea
And threaten to topple the sacred hills.

LORD JING: Fire can dry up water, water can quench fire. It was a brave fight, I'm sure. But who won in the end? My boy has strong magic. He knows many transformations.

MOTHER LIGHTNING: Indeed. His last transformation was into a very small snake.
[*She sings*]   *Gui san tai*

When they hurled themselves forward to attack
The whole world seemed to tremble and reel back,
So great the shock was and so dire.
The sky glowed red with smoke and fire.
Before such force the strongest heart would quail;
Massive iron walls would be of no avail.
But in the end, outmatched, the Young Lord fled.
Then Qiantang, to cut off his retreat,
Winged swiftly upstream over the flood;
At which the Young Lord, flying on ahead,
Concealed himself by burrowing in the mud.

LORD JING: What I want to know is, how did the Princess's family get to hear that she was minding sheep? The Dongting Lake where they live is hundreds of miles from here. How could they possibly know unless someone from here sent word to them?

MOTHER LIGHTNING:
[*She sings*]   *Tiao xiao ling*

It all began with the young, foolish master
Provoking you to banish his princess —
That wretched girl who brought on this disaster.
On the Jing's banks her life was full of care,
Furrowing that brow that once was smooth and fair.

> She wrote a secret record of her griefs
> To send her parents in the lake.
> This letter then, moved by her tearful pleas,
> A passing traveller agreed to take.

I've made inquiries about this passing traveller. It was a young man from Xiangyin* called Liu Yi.

[*She sings*]   *Tu si er*
> The Third Princess was fortune's friend that day,
> Lucky that Liu Yi came her way,
> Lucky that when she told him all,
> He carried her letter to far-away Dongting,
> To the Dragon King of the lake in his Dragon Hall.

LORD JING: So it was a human being who took word to them. How did the family react when they got the message?

MOTHER LIGHTNING:
[*She sings*]   *Sheng yao wang*
> When the king read the letter, anger filled his breast;
> When the Queen heard its message, she was so distressed
> That the sound of her weeping reached Qiantang in his
>   cage.
> The great gold chain that bound him was broken in his
>   rage.
> Like a twig he snapped it and, in his dragon shape,
> High into the sky above he made his escape.

LORD JING: The Qiantang fire dragon may be a very determined opponent, but my son can summon the wind and rain, he has the clouds at his command, he has all those water-troops and goblin warriors too. I can't understand why he should have proved the weaker one of the two.

---

* See footnote on p. 35.

MOTHER LIGHTNING:

[*She sings*]   *Zhuo lu su*

> Our water troops were several thousand strong;
> With goblin warriors they made a mighty throng.
> Unhesitating and unflinching,
> They all pressed forward without fear,
> Turtles and fishes bringing up the rear.
> Valiantly they made a stand.
> Bravely they fought hand to hand.
> But, I fear,
> Death and destruction ended their career.

Yao pian

> What confusion! Some were for flying,
> While wounded all around were lying.
> Surcoats tattered,
> Armour scattered,
> Carved bows shattered,
> Sword-blades battered,
> Standing so close upon the ground
> Scarcely could they turn around.
> Pressed from behind and from above,
> They could only push and shove,
> Till, in the universal slaughter,
> They dropped like buckets in the water.

Shou wei

> Qiantang like flashing lightning showed his might:
> From Baqiao onwards everywhere in sight,
> Dying the waters of the river red,
> Nothing but bobbing corpses of the dead.

LORD JING: [*Deeply distressed*] It seems we are utterly defeated. Tell me then, where is my son?

MOTHER LIGHTNING: Better not ask about him. When the

Qiantang dragon was pursuing him, desperate to escape, he turned himself into a tiny snake and buried himself in the mud. But Qiantang spotted him, dug him out and swallowed him. That's where your poor son ended: in a dragon's belly!

LORD JING: To think that the fate of our river kingdom should be determined by a puny mortal! My son, my princely son, has been brought down by a *man*! But we must endure, we must have patience, we must plan revenge. It will be a slow business, but there will come a time when I shall exterminate that young man and turn the Dongting Lake into a dry plain.

Act Three

SHANG DIAO

NARRATOR: Having disposed of the young dragon of the Jing, Lord Qiantang has conveyed the Third Princess, now a widow, back to the palace beneath Lake Dongting. She thinks fondly of the person who has made her deliverance possible and secretly wishes she could have such a handsome and dependable young man as her husband. Meanwhile her father is preparing a reception for his victorious brother.

[*The Narrator disappears. The scene is now the Dragon Hall of the palace where the whole court is assembled. There are three tables ranged at equal distance from each other on the stage. Those to the right and left have chairs behind them, the centre one, set slightly farther back, is in front of the Dragon King's throne, on which Lord Dongting and his Queen are already seated.*]

LORD DONGTING: [*To the Queen*] I hope Lord Qiantang will behave himself. We owe that young man so much; we don't want to frighten him again.

AN ATTENDANT: [*Announcing*] Lord Qiantang.

[*Enter Lord Qiantang, dressed entirely in red. He is quite young and handsome but looks very fierce. Lord Dongting and the Queen rise to greet him. Lord Qiantang momentarily drops on one knee in deference to his elder brother, then the two brothers exchange greetings, each clasping his own hands, shaking them many times and laughing. He then bows to the Queen, who curtseys back to him.*]

DONGTING: Welcome home! And congratulations!

QIANTANG: It was a great victory, brother.

DONGTING: No one was killed, I hope.

QIANTANG: Oh, about 600,000, I think.

DONGTING: At least I hope you didn't damage the crops.

QIANTANG: There *was* some flooding. About 800 square miles.

DONGTING: And what became of her appalling husband, the young Lord Jing?

QIANTANG: Why do you ask? I ate him.

DONGTING: Now look here, that's all very well; but though he behaved so badly, don't you think that was a little hasty? Suppose His Celestial Majesty gets to hear of this and proves unforgiving? What will you do then?

QIANTANG: I was thinking of *you*, brother. I got so angry, I couldn't help myself.

DONGTING: Well, we'll forget about that for the time being; there's something else I want to discuss with you. We owe that young man who brought the letter to us a great deal. I don't know what would have become of the Princess if it hadn't been for him. I want to do something really fitting to reward him; and since he has already shown himself to be so dependable, I am seriously thinking of offering him my daughter's hand in marriage.

QIANTANG: It will be a very great honour for him if you do. But as you say, brother, you have at least seen what he is like. He would certainly be an improvement on the last husband.

DONGTING: We'll have him in, then. [*To an attendant*] Tell Mr Liu we'd like him to join us in a little celebration.

[*Exit attendant and returns with Liu Yi.*]

DONGTING: Mr Liu, this is my brother, Lord Qiantang. As a matter of fact, you have seen him once already, but in rather less fortunate circumstances and in a different shape.

[*Liu Yi at first looks a little surprised, but then exchanges courtesies with Qiantang.*]

DONGTING: I have been telling Lord Qiantang how grateful we are to you for delivering my daughter's letter. The only adequate way of expressing our gratitude I can think of is to offer you her hand in marriage. Are you willing to become my son-in-law?

LIU YI: [*Looking a little confused and uncertain*] Well, I hardly know what to say. I did what I did because I thought it was right — no more than anyone ought to have done in the circumstances. It would hardly seem right to marry someone when you've just been responsible for bringing about the death of her husband. And in any case, I have a widowed mother who depends entirely on me to look after her. As a matter of fact, she must already be wondering why I haven't returned home yet. I really ought to be taking my leave now, if you will allow me.

QIANTANG: [*Already angry*] You think a Dragon Princess isn't good enough for you? [*Menacingly, drawing much closer*] Listen, little mannikin, we've made this offer and we're asking for a decision. Either you accept, *now*, and everyone will be happy, or it'll be down in the muck together and I'll see to it that you're the one who doesn't get up again.

LIU YI: [*Unflinching and even somewhat disdainfully*] When you're doing your dragon act, shattering chains and pillars, shooting through the air, wreaking havoc and destruction and all the rest of it, I'm impressed by the sheer elemental force. But if you're going to appear in the form of a civilised human being, dressed up in the clothes of an educated man, I don't expect you to go on behaving like a — a *reptile*.

QIANTANG: [*Deflated and instantly contrite*] You have to bear with me, Mr Liu. I was brought up in an underwater palace. I didn't have your educational advantages. Do please accept my apologies. I hope you won't bear me any ill-will for my outburst. [*He clasps hands and bows and Liu Yi does the same in return.*]

DONGTING: That's more like it, brother. I'm sure Mr Liu isn't going to hold anything against you. If he doesn't want to marry the Princess, he doesn't. We can't force him to. Let's call the girl in and get her to thank him herself. But first let's sit down and make ourselves comfortable.

[*He indicates the chair and table to the right of him for Liu Yi to take and the three of them sit down at their separate tables. The Queen, who has all this time been hovering somewhere behind her husband, slips into the seat beside him. He turns to one of the attendants.*] Tell the Third Princess she is to come and meet her benefactor. [*The attendant leaves. Enter the Dragon Princess. She stands at one side in front of the stage, outside an imaginary door. While she sings the following aria, she is invisible to the others inside the hall, who, at the Dragon King's prompting, begin drinking the wine discreetly served them by the attendants.*]

DRAGON PRINCESS:

[*She sings*]   *Ji xian bin*
          My scholar-postman chose the wrong career:
          Examinations weren't for him, I fear.
          And yet, and yet —
          If he'd succeeded in his salmon-leap,
          I'd still be by the river, minding sheep.
          And, as the leap to fame he hoped to make
          Has ended here, beneath the Dongting Lake,
          My dragon-kin should really now decide
          To make him one of us — and me his bride!
[*She raises her skirt and lifts a foot as if stepping over the threshold of an imaginary door.*]
                          Jin ju xiang
          Into the palace hall I go.
          Here at the threshold one's allowed to show,
          Skirt slightly raised, a small amount of toe.
[*She hurries over to her parents and curtseys to them.*]
          First, to my parents dear, I curtsey low,
[*Now she crosses to Lord Qiantang and curtseys to him.*]
          And next to you —
          To you, dear blustering, tempestuous uncle,
          How great a debt I owe!

QIANTANG: [*Laughing*] You owe me nothing, my dear, nothing at all! It was a mere jaunt for me. *You* were the one who had all the trouble.

DONGTING: You would still be in trouble today, daughter, if it weren't for Mr Liu. I think you owe *him* a curtsey, too.

[*Since she came in, Liu Yi has been gazing in rapture at this dazzling apparition. Now, as she approaches him and curtseys, he looks confused and turns his head away. He shakes it sadly as she sings, realising that he has just thrown away the chance of having this beautiful creature as his wife.*]

DRAGON PRINCESS: [*Sings*]

Wu ye er

With little steps I go and hurried pace,
A sleeve demurely hiding half my face,
But taking care to show
A smile of happiness where last time he saw woe.
My curtsey made, I must contrive to say
Some courteous phrases, in the usual way.
"Kind sir, your journey here gave you much trouble;
"It was to help a stranger, too, which makes the
                                        kindness double:
"A stranger who was far from home and in great need:
"A friend like you, sir, is a friend indeed."

[*He hangs his head and says nothing. The Dragon Princess mistakes this for his unwillingness to know her better. In the course of her aria he begins to understand what she is saying, and gazes at her meaningfully.*]

Hou ting hua

Though I'm all eagerness to be his bride,
It seems that he's unwilling to be tied.
The cat has got his tongue: he won't reply,
But steals a glance as if to catch my eye;
And when I frown to show him that I'm hurt,
He looks back tenderly and tries to flirt.
Though outwardly for marriage disinclined,
I think he's inwardly
Of quite a different mind.

LIU YI: A mere mortal, offered a beautiful vision like you! — how *could* I be "disinclined"? I've had to refuse, but I can't help longing for what I know I mustn't have. [*He attempts to take her hand.*]

DRAGON PRINCESS: [*Continuing her aria*]

> My uncle's watching, you had best take care:
> You're really in for it if he's aware.
> His roar of rage is like the tempest's blast;
> When he breathes smoke, the sky grows overcast.
> His warning growl would cause your soul to flit;
> Your body, at his slightest touch, would split.
> How fierce he can be you would quickly find,
> Though normally so gentle and so kind.

LIU YI: I have a widowed mother to think about. And in any case, it's not very nice planning to marry someone when you're more or less responsible for their husband's death. I've *had* to refuse.

DRAGON PRINCESS: [*Sings*]

> *Liu ye er*
>
> Scholar, it's beyond debate,
> A home is no home if you're celibate.
> You'll find it hard, so hard, to live in
>   single state.
> Must you really condemn yourself to such
>   a dreary fate?
> You're so good-natured, scholar, and so true,
> No woman could refuse a man like you.

[*Liu Yi gazes very languishingly at the Princess. The Princess, accepting that she cannot have him, picks up a wine-kettle in a businesslike manner and begins pouring wine for him.*]

DRAGON PRINCESS: [*She sings*]

> *Cu hu lu*
>
> We shan't be tasting married bliss in bed;
> I'll have to be his hostess, then, instead.
> I'm very much afraid, though,

Before the wine has touched his lips,
That already something else
Has gone to his head.

LORD DONGTING: We have arranged this little family party as a
means of expressing our gratitude to Mr Liu. Let us first drink a health
to him and then I shall myself join in performing a little offering I have
prepared in his honour.

[*After they have all drained a cup, he claps his hands and a little group of
two or three musicians appears together with a troupe of half a dozen or so
dancers. The musicians sit on stools and the dancers take up their positions
and, when the music starts, begin dancing, more or less statically. While the
Dragon King intones the following ode in a voice somewhere between singing
and chanting, the musicians accompany him with a very sparse sort of music in
which the beat of the clappers or of a wooden block predominates.*]

Good marriages are made in heaven
But hers was not to be for life
We meant well, but the one she wed
Was no fit match for such a wife

On the bleak northern riverside
In loneliness she nursed her pain
Chilled by each passing wind that blew
Or soaked and shivering in the rain

But now our dear one, thanks to you,
Is with us as she was before
We'll bless you for this evermore (*bis*)

[*When the performance has ended, Liu Yi rises to his feet and bows to
Lord Dongting. Lord Dongting raises his winecup and he and Liu Yi drink
to each other.*]
QIANTANG: What do you call that piece?
DONGTING: I thought of calling it "The Princess's Joyful return".
DRAGON PRINCESS: [*Ruefully. She is still singing to the "Cu hu lu"
tune.*]

"The Princess's Joyful Return", did you say?
The man I might have married is allowed to walk away.
Lord Dongting, oh, Lord Dongting,
This is *not* a joyful day!

QIANTANG: Pour me another drink, niece. *I've* got a contribution,
too.

[*The Dragon Princess pours for him and he quickly gulps down a
cupful before standing up and striking a pose. The musicians accompany
him and the dancers dance while he intones, but this time much more
vigorously and dramatically.*]

> Beneath the blue and boundless sky
> Within the vast encircling sea
> Who can predict what any man
> Will in the end turn out to be?
>
> Snug in their holes like mice and rats
> The wicked may feel free from care
> But when the Avenger finds them out
> His lightning strikes them even there
>
> Good friend, because you kept your word
> Our dear one's with us here today
> This kindness nothing can repay (*bis*)

[*Liu Yi rises and bows to Qiantang and the two of them drink to each
other.*]

DONGTING: What do you call *your* contribution, brother?
QIANTANG: I call it "Qiantang Breaks the Foemen's Ranks".
DONGTING: Very stirring. "The winds and waters echo the refrain,"
you might say. — Where does that come from, by the way?
DRAGON PRINCESS: [*Sings*]

> *Jin ju xiang*
> "The winds and waters echo the refrain."
> My Uncle Qiantang is a little vain,
> No doubt we'll hear that many times again.

QIANTANG: [*To Liu Yi, confidentially*] You know, scholar, I don't know why you didn't accept our offer. It really would be quite an honour for you to marry the Princess.

DRAGON PRINCESS: [*To the same tune*]
> Uncle, as matchmaker you're a disgrace.
> Your contributions are so out of place.

LIU YI: [*Rising*] I am more grateful than I can say for this entertainment, but I fear the time has come when I really must take my leave.

DRAGON PRINCESS: If you must go now, at least let us give you a parting gift to take with you. [*To the attendants*] Bring the presents for Mr Liu.

[*Exeunt attendants and return laden with caskets and precious objects. The Princess sings.*]

Lang li lai sha

> These worthless gifts, sir, you must not refuse.
> Think of them as a letter-bearer's dues.

[*Liu Yi rises and goes to each of the other three, bowing his farewells. An attendant comes in with his satchel and hangs it on his shoulder for him. He moves to go, the gift-bearers in attendance. The Princess continues singing to the same tune.*]

> Our marriage offer you reject
> All from a stupid wish to be correct.
> And so, for both of us, our hopes of happiness
> Are wrecked.

[*Liu Yi takes his leave of the Princess. As he is going she sings to the same tune.*]

> Now I go to my lonely palace room,
> While you, in some cottage far away,
> Must pass your nights in solitary gloom.

[*Exit*]

DONGTING: I don't think we handled that very well. We shall have to see if another opportunity ever arises of rewarding that young man properly.

QIANTANG: I can see I'm not a very good matchmaker. I'd gladly do something to make amends.

Act Four

SHUANG DIAO

[*The Narrator appears with two figures, one seated, one standing, on either side of him. The standing one is Liu Yi and the seated one is old Mrs Liu as in Act One. At first we are only aware of the Narrator.*]

NARRATOR: After his homecoming and the humiliation of having to announce his failure to his mother and disappoint her hopes, Liu Yi travelled with the presents the dragon people had given him to the nearest city where there was a market for gold and gems. He found that what he had been given was no fairy gold but the real thing, and even after the deduction of an exorbitant charge for the valuation, the sale was enough to make him a very rich man. On his return he and his mother were able to move into a large house, buy expensive new clothes and furniture, and still have a comfortable amount left to live on. Old Mrs Liu could satisfy her long-cherished ambition to get a wife for her son: a girl who would provide an heir for the family and look after her in her old age. Now, with the help of a matchmaker, she thinks she has found one.

[*The Narrator fades. We become aware that the two figures to left and right of him are Liu Yi and his mother, both better dressed that when we saw them last.*]

MRS LIU: Lately I've been thinking a lot about your future, my son, and I have at last succeeded in arranging a marriage for you. The girl I've chosen is a Miss Lu from the Lu family of Fanyang. It's a very good family, but the father is dead and the mother is remarrying. The calendar shows that it's a lucky day for weddings, so I've asked the matchmaker to bring her along tomorrow. I want you to be ready for her.

LIU YI: I know it's my duty to obey you, mother, but I can't help thinking about that Third Princess. She wanted me to be her husband, you know, and her father the Dragon King himself asked me if I would like to be his son-in-law. At the time I refused, of course, but I should find it very, very hard to be married to anyone else.

MRS LIU: You mustn't think like that, my son, it isn't healthy. Just do what your mother tells you.

LIU YI: [*Looking very miserable*] Yes, mother.

   [*They disappear, and the Narrator appears again.*]

NARRATOR: After Liu Yi left the palace under the lake, the Dragon Princess became more and more dejected, until her parents began to fear that she would pine away. Discovering, by supernatural means, that the young man's mother was making plans for her son to marry, they agreed to a ruse whereby their daughter would enter the human world as a mortal and offer herself as a suitable bride. The Miss Lu of Fanyang chosen for her son by Mrs Liu was a fiction. She was in fact none other than the Dragon Princess in disguise. We shall see her presently, arriving outside the Lius' house on the day of the wedding.

   [*The Narrator disappears and the pseudo Miss Lu and the Matchmaker, who is a middle-aged woman, enter in two small sedan chairs and dismount. Two large red lanterns are hanging up to indicate that this is a wedding.*]

DRAGON PRINCESS: [*Sings*]
                    Xin shui ling
        In a double lotus-plant, when it's divided,
        Long filaments survive the root's bisection:
        So are the hearts of separated lovers.
        My filaments now float in the right direction.
        Though, when we met, he hadn't much to say,
        I'm sure he missed me when he went away.
        He's no conception how a girl needs tending.
        I hope he's not still starchy and unbending.

[*Strains of wedding music are heard from inside the house, so-na and cymbals predominating.*]

DRAGON PRINCESS: What sound is that?

MATCHMAKER: That's the wedding music. They're playing for your wedding.

DRAGON PRINCESS: [*Sings*]

Zhu ma ting

Bright wedding-lights hung high in celebration:
It was for you I underwent
This transformation.
Gay music that I ought to hear with gladness:
Time was you brought me only sadness.
Far from my watery home, the dragon's exiled
daughter:
Strange he should meet me there, beside that other
water!
My heart misgives me: what if those gentle eyes
Should fail to know me in this mortal guise?

[*The Matchmaker drapes a semi-transparent red cloth over the Princess's head, completely covering her face. The scene changes to inside the house. Mrs Liu is seated with Liu Yi standing beside her. His hat is decorated with a red wedding-favour. Liu Yi advances to meet the Princess and Matchmaker as they enter. The Matchmaker ushers him and the Princess into the middle of the stage, facing Mrs Liu, who is seated to one side of it. She goes up to Mrs Liu, curtseys and appears momentarily to be conferring with her. Then she takes up a position to conduct the ceremony.*]

MATCHMAKER: Bride and groom, kowtow to Heaven.

[*Liu Yi and the Dragon Princess face upstage with their backs to the audience and kowtow.*]

MATCHMAKER: Bride and groom, kowtow to Earth.

[*They face the audience and kowtow.*]

MATCHMAKER: Bride and groom, kowtow to the groom's Mother.

[*They face Mrs Liu and kowtow.*]

MATCHMAKER: Bride and groom, kowtow to each other.

[*They face inwards towards each other and kowtow. When they have both stood up, Liu Yi raises the red cloth from the Princess's face and looks at her. He appears surprised.*]

LIU YI: [*As if to himself*] It's strange: this girl's face seems so familiar. [*He addresses the Matchmaker.*] *Where* did you say this girl comes from?

MATCHMAKER: She's from Fanyang. The Lu family of Fanyang.

LIU YI: Her father is dead, I know; but what was he when he was alive.

MATCHMAKER: I can't tell you much about him. Something to do with fish, I think. He was very rich and influential.

LIU YI: I wonder where I could have met her in the past. I just have this feeling that I have seen her somewhere before.

DRAGON PRINCESS: [*Sings*]

Ye xing chuan

He seems most anxious to know everything.
We did once meet, beside the River Jing.
But if I told him all, I fear that it would seem,
To mortal ears, fantastical
In the extreme.
The King of Chu might think
The goddess he met face to face
Was just a dream.

[*Turning to Liu Yi and addressing him*] Mr Liu, do you really not remember me?

LIU YI: Well, I don't see how I can. Your face reminds me of somebody, but I don't think we can ever have met before.

DRAGON PRINCESS: [*Sings*]

Gu mei jiu

When I was a lonely slave and shepherdess,
You pitied me in my distress.
You took the letter

That freed me from a life of servitude.
How to repay that debt of gratitude,
What means I'd find your kindness to requite:
I could think of nothing else
Both day and night.

LIU YI: Is it possible? Can you be her?

DRAGON PRINCESS: [*Sings*]
Tai ping ling
Don't you remember the banks of the River Jing?
I am the Third Princess, daughter of the Dragon King —
She of the woeful face and tousled head,
Whom you did not expect, I'm sure,
To share with you one day a bridal bed.
But come, today's a lucky day, a day of joy and
laughter,
Come with me to my home beneath the water!

LIU YI: [*Excitedly*] Mother, this bride you chose for me wasn't Miss
Lu from Fanyang. This is the Third Princess, the daughter of the
Dragon King whom I delivered the letter for and then met in the palace
at the bottom of Lake Dongting. She wants us to go there with her to
meet her parents.

MRS LIU: Bless my soul! What a lucky young man you are!

DRAGON PRINCESS: Mr Liu, that time I met you on the banks of
the Jing and you promised to deliver my letter, why, when you were
leaving, did you tell me that if I ever got back to the lake and you
wanted to visit me there, I was not to avoid seeing you?

LIU YI: I was joking. I didn't mean anything serious. I thought that
if you got back to the lake, you would probably forget all about me.

DRAGON PRINCESS: [*Sings*]
Yan er luo
You were my saviour, how could I forget?
You plucked me from misfortune's net.

When I invented this high-born Miss Lu,
Dear friend in need, it was to marry you!

[*She speaks.*] Will you come with me, then?

LIU YI: I don't know how we mortal creatures are to get into your world, but if you can show us how, I'm willing to go with you.

DRAGON PRINCESS: [*Sings*]
                    De sheng ling
Come, then!
Drunk on the wine of immortality, we'll ride,
Each of us an immortal, side by side.

[*She takes a position forward from the rest and stands with outstretched arms, looking upwards. There is a strange, vibrating sound suggesting that a potent magic is at work, continuous, but not loud enough to drown out sung or spoken speech. There is darkness with flashes of light in which we can barely see the three figures — the Match-maker having disappeared by now — standing together, possibly moving very slowly forwards and upwards as if on an escalator, if this can be contrived.*]

See, where a rainbow bridge in the sky appears!
Like the Lanqiao Bridge, it leads to the fairy world.
[*Sound of breakers*]
Let me support you, mother:
It's the roar of breakers that sounds now in your
                                                    ears:
We're passing where the sun first rises from the sea.
[*Here the sound changes to soothing harplike music*]
And now we're nearing Dongting:
I can smell
The blossom of the lakeside orange-tree.

[*The music ends, the figures disappear, and the scene changes to a formal tableau. This is the Dragon Hall, but now in the centre is a large curtained Chinese bed. There are wedding scrolls and lanterns symmetrically*] *arranged. Lord Dongting, the Queen and members of their court are waiting. Enter Mrs Liu and the newly married pair.*]

DONGTING: [*To Mrs Liu*] Welcome, kinswoman! [*Mrs Liu curtseys.*] Welcome again and congratulations, son-in-law. [*Liu Yi bows. He turns to his daughter.*] Are you happy now? [*For some reason the entire company think this very funny.*]

DRAGON PRINCESS: [*Sings*]
Yuan yang wei sha
Rescued in rags from troubled waters,
Back in the silken luxury of the Dongting Lake,
I thought when I met you there you would surely
claim me,
But your silly scruples taught me my mistake.
You left me to soak my handkerchiefs with tears
And dance and song and all my joys forsake.
But here, today, my faithful scholar,
You plight a troth that nothing now can shake.
[*She and Liu Yi are by now standing shoulder to shoulder in front of the curtained bed.*]
Our tale concludes by a marriage bed's rich hangings,
Where we await the triumphs of the night.
Immortalised in prose, this pretty story
Is here reshaped and shown for your delight.
[*Lord Dongting now steps forward and addresses the audience from the centre of the stage.*]
DONGTING: [*Reciting*]
All creatures share with man a common fate
Assigning each one his allotted mate;
And wedlock, once rejected, now attained,
Proves that this couple's match was preordained.
The lack of good faith is as great disgrace
In birds and beasts as in the human race;
And when you men behave with rectitude,

We water-creatures, too, feel gratitude.
Thus ends our story of the Third Princess
And Scholar Liu who pitied her distress.

Appendix

"Padding Words" in the Lyrics of Yuan *Zaju*

In my translation of this *zaju* I have deliberately refrained from translating the titles of the song-tunes to which the lyrics were set (*Dian jiang chun*, *Tian xia le*, etc.) because to have done so would have been misleading. They were appropriate to the songs that were originally sung to those tunes, but are irrelevant to the lyrics set to them by the playwrights just as the titles of the song-tunes Gay used in his "Beggar's Opera" are irrelevant to the words of his libretto.

There are a few exceptions, like the group of lyrics entitled *Yi ban er* (一半兒) or "One Half", in which some residual element of the original song has survived. In *Yi ban er* the last line always contains the words "… *yi ban er* xx *yi ban er* x". For example, there is a play called "The Tiger-Head Tally" (虎頭牌) by the Khitan playwright Li Zhifu (李直夫) in which a capable young commander unwisely offers an important commission to his alcoholic uncle. While the uncle, who knows he ought to refuse the offer but finds it hard to resist, is hesitating, the young man sings an *Yi ban er* lyric which ends

我見他一半兒推辭一半兒肯
I can see he's half trying to refuse and half consenting.

In another play called "Taoist Master Zhang" (張天師) it is said of someone

元來是一半兒裝呆一半兒懂
Really he's half acting stupid and half understanding.

But such examples in which the title of a tune is relevant to the words of the lyrics are extremely rare and are, I think, best ignored.

I shall be attempting in this Appendix to give some idea of the metrical structure of *zaju* lyrics, with particular reference to the use of *chenzi* (襯字) or "padding words" already briefly referred to on pp. 5–6, by taking a single short lyric, the *Tian xia le* (天下樂) from Act One (pp. 37–38), and comparing it with *Tian xia le* lyrics selected from eight other plays, two of them by Shang Zhongxian himself, one by the doyen of Yuan *zaju* writers, Guan Hanqing, and the rest by the equally famous playwright Wang Shifu.

I have listed all nine plays, the "Dragon Princess" and the other eight, in the following table, assigning each of them a letter, from A to I, for ease of reference and giving, after the names of the playwrights, (1) their full Chinese titles, (2) the shorter titles by which they are generally known, and (3) my own English titles for them. This will be followed first by synopses of the eight plays from B to I, then, on pp. 86–94, by the Chinese texts of all nine *Tian xia le* lyrics from A to I with rhythmically stressed parts clearly differentiated from the unstressed "padding" and with both literal and paraphrased translations of the words. Finally, in order to make comparison easier, I shall examine *Tian xia le* line by line, collecting all examples of the line on a single page so that their differences can be clearly seen.

It will be found that there are six lines in a *Tian xia le* lyric. As to the rhyme scheme: *zaju* playwrights used the same rhyme throughout a whole act, only changing the rhyme with the change of key or mode in another act; the only variation allowed is the alternation of rhymed and unrhymed lines. In a *Tian xia le* lyric all the lines rhyme except the fourth, in which rhyme is optional. In seven of the lyrics selected here the fourth line is unrhymed. The two with rhyme in the fourth line, G and I, are by Wang Shifu; but E, F and H, in which the fourth lines are unrhymed, are also by Wang Shifu, so the choice is arbitrary rather than idiosyncratic.

	Playwright	Long Title	Short Title	My Title
A	尚仲賢 Shang Zhongxian	洞庭湖柳毅傳書 In Lake Dongting Liu Yi Delivers a Letter	柳毅傳書	Liu Yi and the Dragon Princess
B	"	尉遲恭三奪槊 Yuchi Gong Three Times Snatches the Lance	三奪槊	Yuchi Thrice Takes the Lance
C	"	漢高皇濯足氣英布 Emperor Gao of Han Enrages Ying Bu by Washing His Feet	氣英布	A Studied Insult
D	關漢卿 Guan Hanqing	感天地竇娥冤 Heaven and Earth Are Moved by Dou E's Wrongs	竇娥冤	Snow in Summer
E– G	王實甫 Wang Shifu	崔鶯鶯待月西廂記 Cui Yingying Awaits the Moon in the Western Chamber	西廂記	The Western Chamber
E	"	(1) 張君瑞鬧道場 Zhang Junrui Causes a Riot in the Requiem	鬧道場	Riot in the Requiem
F	"	(3) 張君瑞害相思 Zhang Junrui Suffers from Lovesickness	害相思	The Lover's Sickness
G	"	(4) 草橋店夢鶯鶯 Dreaming of Yingying in the Hay Bridge Inn	夢鶯鶯	Dreaming of Yingying
H	"	呂蒙正風雪破窰記 Lu Mengzheng's Ruined Cave-house in a Blizzard	破窰記	The Hovel in a Hole
I	"	韓彩雲絲竹芙蓉亭 Han Caiyun Makes Music in the Hibiscus Pavilion	芙蓉亭	The Hibiscus Pavilion

SYNOPSES

B

YUCHI THRICE TAKES THE LANCE

The action of this play is based on an apocryphal version of events in the life of an historical person: Yuchi Jingde (538–658), one of the generals who helped Li Shimin, the future emperor Taizong of the Tang dynasty, to establish his family's control over the whole of China in the period of anarchy following the collapse of the short-lived Sui dynasty. He was one of the Twenty-four Worthies whose likenesses Taizong caused to be preserved in the Lingyan Pavilion in recognition of their services to the dynasty.

Yuchi originally fought under the banner of another warlord and only surrendered to Li Shimin when all the other forces on his side had been decisively beaten. Once he had surrendered, however, he served Li Shimin faithfully and Li Shimin always trusted him, but some of the other Tang generals suspected him of disloyalty and even on one occasion, succeeded in having him imprisoned.

Yuchi's weapon of choice was a formidable "whip" of jointed steel and his most famous accomplishment the ability to dodge a lance aimed at him by a charging horseman while simultaneously wresting it from his grasp. On one occasion he successfully demonstrated this ability to Li Shimin's disbelieving younger brother Li Yuanji, much to the latter's chagrin.

Except for a short exchange between two of the play's characters in the few lines of introduction which precede Act One, the Chinese text of this play contains no dialogue or stage directions whatever. It is a *mo* play with an all-male cast. Fortunately there is a note at the beginning of each act indicating which role the *mo* is singing in that act. Even so, with only the lyrics to go by it is difficult to get more than a rough idea of the play's action.

There is another play about Yuchi Jingde, this one by Guan Hanqing, the author of D. The Chinese text of Guan's play contains both dialogue and stage directions, so there are no difficulties in understanding its action. Both plays, Shang Zhongxian's and Guan Hanqing's, refer to the same two incidents, the battle of Meiliang Brook and the rescue in the Yuke Garden. The battle of Meiliang Brook was where Yuchi, still in the service of another warlord, was defeated by one of Li Shimin's generals. He and his beaten army retreated to the town of Jiexiu and were besieged there by Li Shimin, to whom he eventually surrendered. The Yuke Garden was where Li Shimin was cornered after a long and exhausting flight from an enemy who had caught him unprepared. He was saved there from almost certain death by the arrival in the nick of time of the recently-surrendered Yuchi who had no time to saddle his horse or put on armour and was armed only with his famous "whip".

Guan's play begins with Yuchi besieged by Li Shimin in Jiexiu and ends with his heroic rescue of Li Shimin in the Yuke Garden. When Shang's play begins, the battle of Meiliang Brook and the rescue in the Yuke Garden are both in the past. It appears to end with a re-enactment of the Yuke Garden rescue in an arena for the entertainment of the emperor. (In both plays the Tang emperor is Li Shimin's father, Li Yuan, who reigned from 618 until Li Shimin's accession in 627.)

In both of these plays Li Shimin's younger brother Li Yuanji is portrayed as a scheming villain, but whereas in Guan's play his implacable hatred of Yuchi is due to the fact that he had been wounded by Yuchi's "whip" in the battle of Meiliang Brook, in Shang's play it is because he is plotting to displace Li Shimin as Li Yuan's successor and regards Yuchi as the chief obstacle to his success.

In the *Tian xia le* from Act One of Shang Zhongxian's "Yuchi Thrice Takes the Lance" the role taken by the *mo* is that of Liu Wenjing, the officer on Li Shimin's staff who defeated Yuchi in the battle of Meiliang Brook. Yuchi is now himself a trusted member of Li Shimin's staff, but Li Yuanji plots to engineer his fall by showing a painting of the Battle of Meiliang Brook to his father the Emperor in which Yuchi is vividly portrayed wreaking havoc in the Tang ranks. He charges Yuchi with disloyalty, so enraging the Emperor that he orders

Yuchi's instant arrest and punishment. However, Liu Wenjing, forewarned, has brought another painting to show the Emperor: a vivid representation of Yuchi's heroic rescue of Li Shimin in the Yuke Garden.

In the aria Liu Wenjing laments the fact that the real authors of Tang's success were all distinguished soldiers originally fighting for other warlords who were won over to the Tang cause by Li Shimin's astuteness and diplomatic tact, yet now that peace has come and civilian members of the govemment are doing so well for themselves, these loyal soldiers, survivors of many battles and scarred with many wounds, have the headsman's axe to look forward to as their reward.

C
A STUDIED INSULT

This is another historical drama by Shang Zhongxian. The setting, like that of "Yuchi Thrice Takes the Lance", is the power struggle following the break-up of unified order under an effective but short-lived dynasty and ending with the re-unification of the empire and the establishment of a long-lasting dynasty by the victorious survivor. In this case it was the Qin empire which began to fall apart in the last years of the third century B.C. and the Han dynasty (202 B.C.–A.D. 220) which was founded by the victorious Liu Bang, or "King of Han" as he was called in the period in which the action of this play is set.

The play is set at a point in the life-and-death struggle between the two principal survivors of the civil war: Liu Bang, the King of Han, and Xiang Yu, the King of Chu. Liu Bang is a rude peasant who sometimes shows his contempt for educated civilians by snatching off their hats and pissing in them, whereas Xiang Yu, though an irascible and violent man, is an aristocrat and capable of noble sentiments.

When the play opens, Xiang Yu is preoccupied with a campaign in the North-East and Liu Bang is anxious to win over his most able general Ying Bu, at present stationed with a large force in Central China and already suspected of disloyalty by Xiang Yu because of slanders put about by a rival general. If Liu Bang can win Ying Bu's support and involve him in a plan that he has already worked out for Xiang Yu's encirclement, he is sure that the end of this war is in sight. Sui He, a trained rhetorician who is an undistinguished civilian member of Liu Bang's staff, volunteers to go to Ying Bu's camp with only a tiny escort and persuade him to defect. He and Ying Bu came from the same village, he says, and when they were boys he was Ying Bu's best friend.

Sui He does succeed in inducing Ying Bu to defect by a series of cruel tricks, including the murder of an envoy from Xiang Yu, but when Ying Bu approaches the encampment of the King of Han, instead of the welcoming party and rewards and honours that Sui He had promised, his arrival is totally ignored; and when he finally goes to call on Liu Bang in his tent, he finds him sprawled on a camp-bed having his feet washed by a couple of maids. Ying Bu's anger gives way to despair. Restrained with some difficulty from committing suicide, he is planning to abandon the fighting for a life of banditry when preparations for a feast are brought to his tent followed by visits from all Liu Bang's senior staff and finally by the King of Han himself, who kneels to Ying Bu in the course of a ceremony of investiture and then drinks with him until he is intoxicated and has to be carried back to his camp, leaving a grateful Ying Bu resolved to set off at once to attack his former commander.

Sui He had previously attempted to explain Liu Bang's insulting behaviour by saying that he had been wounded in the foot in an earlier engagement, and that in any case he had always, since his youth, suffered from smelly feet that required frequent washing; but Liu Bang himself explains that the insult was deliberate. He had wanted to make it clear to Ying Bu that any honours he received were not a payment for having transferred his allegiance but a token of the rewards that would be earned by future services.

In this play the *mo* represents Ying Bu in Acts One, Two and Three. In Act Four he appears as the messenger who reports on Ying Bu's victory over Xiang Yu to the King of Han. This is rather like the second act of the "Dragon Princess" in which a messenger (Mother Lightning) describes the battle between the dragons. Interestingly enough Guan Hanqing's play about Yuchi also devotes a whole act to narration by a messenger.

D
SNOW IN SUMMER

This is the most famous play by Guan Hanqing, who is considered to be the greatest of the Yuan *zaju* writers. Unlike the other plays cited in this Appendix, its action concerns the lives of lower-class people of Guan's own day.

The two female characters in this play are Mrs Cai, a small trader's widow with an eight-year-old son who makes a living as a money-lender, and Dou E, the motherless daughter of an impecunious scholar who is one of Mrs Cai's debtors. When it becomes apparent that Dou E's father will never be able to pay back what he owes, Mrs Cai offers to cancel the loan and in addition to give him a sum of money that will enable him to travel to the capital and compete in the civil service examinations if in return he will hand over Dou E to be a domestic help for her and a future wife for her little boy. The scholar perforce accepts and takes a sorrowful leave of his daughter. End of Prologue.

At the beginning of Act One Dou E has been living with Mrs Cai for a number of years, in the course of which she had married the son, a weakly young man who had died shortly after the marriage, and is now resigned, at the age of twenty, to living with Mrs Cai as a widowed daughter-in-law. During all these years not a word has been heard from her father.

On this particular day Mrs Cai is out collecting debts. One of her debtors is an incompetent physician living outside the city who despairs of ever being able to pay back his debt and has resolved to free himself of it by violent means. When the old woman calls at his house, he tells her that the money is at his place of work and inveigles her into accompanying him to a lonely spot where he takes out a cord and proceeds to strangle her. Her cries bring an old man and his son running to her aid. The physician takes to his heels and the new arrivals revive her. When they learn that she is a widow with some money who has a young widowed daughter-in-law living with her, they foresee a comfortable life for themselves if they can persuade the two women to become their wives, and when Mrs Cai objects, they threaten to finish off the job that had been started by the physician unless she will comply. She consents to take the precious pair back to her house, saying that she cannot answer for her daughter-in-law but will do what she can to talk her into accepting the young man as her husband.

Dou E of course indignantly rejects all attempts to win her over, and a situation develops in which the older couple are living as man and wife, while Dou E spends much of her time warding off the attentions of the son. When Mrs Cai falls ill, the son decides to poison her, thereby robbing Dou E of her last defence. He happens, by coincidence, to purchase the poison he uses from an apothecary-shop outside the city where Mrs Cai's would-be assassin the physician is now making a living. He slips it into some soup that Dou E has prepared for her mother-in-law, but the old lady declines to take it immediately and it is mistakenly eaten, with fatal results, by the father.

Still refusing to yield to the young man's importunity, Dou E is dragged off to the magistrate's court and accused of murdering her "father". She refuses to confess when tortured, but finally agrees to do so when Mrs Cai too is threatend with torture. Condemned to death by beheading, she protests her innocence at the place of execution, saying that she will demonstrate it by three signs: (1) the blood from her decapitated head will fly upwards towards a nearby banner, (2) snow will fall out of the summer sky and (3) there will be three years of drought.

Dou E's father now finally makes an appearance. He has been made Commissioner of Justice for the province and Dou E's is one of the many cases he has to review. With a little help from his daughter's ghost, he gets to the bottom of it, the guilty are punished, and Dou E, rather late in the day and not very satisfactorily, one would have thought, is vindicated.

This is a *dan* play. The *dan* takes the part of Dou E throughout.

E, F, G
THE WESTERN CHAMBER

This is the best-known Yuan *zaju*, probably the best-known Chinese drama of any kind, having gone into countless Chinese editions and been translated into a number of foreign languages.

Strictly speaking, it is not one *zaju* but five, which makes it, in effect, a twenty-act play. It is also exceptional among Yuan *zaju* in requiring more than one singer in three of the five plays. Only the first and third conform to the normal pattern by requiring only one singer, a *mo* and *dan* respectively, throughout.

Each of the five *zaju* has a separate title of its own, though these are not often used, as it is customary to refer to all of them by their collective title. The lyrics cited in this Appendix are from the first, third and fourth of the five plays: viz. (E) "Riot in the Requiem", (F) "The Lover's Sickness" and (G) "Dreaming of Yingying".

Like "The Dragon Princess", "The Western Chamber" is based on an elegantly-written prose story by a Tang writer, in this case Yuan Zhen (779–831), life-long friend and correspondent of the poet Bai Juyi (Po Chü-i) and himself a well-known poet. Yuan Zhen's story is thought to be autobiographical, a thinly-disguised account of an episode dating from his student days, describing his sexual initiation in the course of a passionate affair with a young woman he met in his travels and his subsequent abandonment of her. In an attempt to meet her some years later when she was a married woman, he was even less successful than Pushkin's hero, for she refused to see him.

Yuan Zhen's portrait of his heroine Yingying ("Oriole") has a mysterious, elusive quality, fascinating to susceptible male readers. The story was an instant success, and in numerous dramatisations, mostly with a happy ending attached, it has become the supreme example of romantic love in Chinese literature. Wang Shifu's *zaju* sequence is little more than a recycling of an earlier musical version designed for a solo performance in which singing and spoken narrative were combined.

In Wang's "Western Chamber" Yingying is a young woman of

good family travelling with her widowed mother and maid Hongniang, temporarily lodging in a monastery where the scholar Zhang is also lodging. During their stay the monastery is threatened by armed bandits and Yingying's mother offers her daughter's hand in marriage to whoever can save them. However, when Zhang does so by getting a message through to a local military commander who happens to be a friend of his, she reneges on her promise and finds another way of rewarding him. Zhang has already seen something of Yingying and fallen for her charms. He finds an ally in the maid Hongniang, who has been made indignant by the duplicity of her senior mistress, and with the help of moonlight, music, poetry and the wiles of the good-natured maid, the two lovers are finally brought to bed. Eventually their secret gets out, there are scenes, tears and partings and Yingying is nearly married to another man; but in the end, in a not very highly-regarded sequel, Zhang triumphs in the civil service examinations and the couple are reunited and married.

H
THE HOVEL IN A HOLE

In this play a wealthy man whose only child is a daughter decides to solve the problem of choosing a husband for her by having a colourful "tower" constructed — a temporary wooden structure covered with embroidered hangings — and getting the girl, attended by her maid, to stand on top of it and throw an embroidered silken ball to the assembled suitors below. Whoever the ball lands on will be the lucky man. He has second thoughts about the wisdom of his idea when the ball lights on an impoverished scholar who lives in a cave-dwelling outside the city (the "hovel in a hole" of the *zaju*'s title) and ekes out a beggar-like existence on the city streets. The girl insists on marrying him despite all remonstrations, so angering her father that he turns her out of doors and disowns her. She endures years of poverty and hardship until her husband comes out top in the Imperial examinations. Riches and honours soon follow and the tower-top choice is vindicated.

The male lead in this play is an historical person, Lü Mengzheng (946–1011), who rose to eminence from very impoverished beginnings and for some years really did live in a cave-dwelling; but the story of the ball thrown from a tower is a fiction that turns up elsewhere. Some readers may have encountered an English version of it in S. I. Hsiung's "Lady Precious Stream", an adaptation of the Peking drama *Wang Bao Chuan.*

"The Hovel in a Hole" is a *dan* play in which the singing role in each of the four acts (there is no prologue or interlude) is that of the rich man's daughter. Her father is a "Mr Liu", but she herself remains anonymous throughout. At the point in Act One where this lyric occurs she is standing on the tower discussing with her maid the relative merits of the young men who are standing below, waiting for her to throw the ball. The maid suggests that she should throw it to one of the better-dressed ones, not to some half-starved looking scholar; but Miss Liu objects that many great men have come from poor backgrounds and cites several examples from history. Her final example is an ancient one in every sense: Lü Wang, chief adviser to the Zhou dynastic founder King Wen, was still, at eighty years old, a poor fisherman when King Wen discovered him.

"Wouldn't you be a bit old by then?" asks the maid innocently.

The *Tian xia le* lyric is her mistress's reply. Hence the first line: "Good fortune doesn't come in a hurry."

I

THE HIBISCUS PAVILION

Apart from the title, this play by Wang Shifu survives only as a fragment: fourteen lyrics in the *Xian lü* mode. There are no stage directions or indications of role or singer. There is not even any mention of the act it belongs to, though we can assume that it is the first act because Yuan *zaju* writers almost invariably use the *Xian lü* mode for the first act. And we can be confident that it is the *whole* sung part of Act One because the first lyric is a *Dian jiang chun*, with which a *Xian lü* sequence invariably begins (cf. p. 36), and the last one is a *Wei sheng*, which is the commonest kind of coda.

From the lyrics it would appear that the person singing is a female, the "Han Caiyun" of the title looks like a girl's name, and a chance reference in a lyric by another (anonymous) Yuan playwright makes it seem likely that the story, otherwise unknown, on which this play is based is about an affair between a girl called Han Caiyun and a young man called Cui Boying. So this is a *dan* play and the character singing in these lyrics is the Han Caiyun of the title.

In the *Tian xia le* lyric she appears to have stolen into a moonlit courtyard and up to the room in which Cui Boying is studying. There has clearly been a misunderstanding. She is under the impression that she will be welcomed inside, but the young man coldly ignores her and she finally departs, feeling ashamed and humiliated. Daiyu experiences a similar sense of desolation when she finds herself shut out of Baoyu's courtyard in the twenty-sixth chapter of the *Story of the Stone*.

This is the reverse of the situation in "The Western Chamber" in which Yingying, having at first coldly rejected Zhang's advances, voluntarily steals over to his apartment at night to offer herself to him and is rapturously received.

CHINESE TEXTS

A
LIU YI AND THE DRAGON PRINCESS

1. 俺家在南天水國居   (7)*
An JIA / ZAI NAN TIAN / SHUI GUO / JU
My family / in southern sky / water kingdom / live

2. 就兒裏非無尺素書   (5)
JIU er LI / fei wu / CHI SU SHU
Inside here / not lack / length of silk letter

3. 奈衡陽不傳鴻雁羽   (7)
Nai / HENG YANG / BU CHUAN / HONG YAN YU
Unfortunately / Hengyang / not deliver / wild goose wing

4. 黃犬又筋力疲   (5)
HUANG QUAN / you / JIN LI / PI
Brown dog / also / muscle strength / exhausted

5. 錦鱗又性格愚   (5)
JIN LIN / you / XING GE / YU
Gilded scales / also / nature / stupid

6. 幾遍家待相通常間阻   (5)
Ji bian jia dai / XIANG TONG / CHANG / JIAN ZU
How many times wait / communication / always / blocked

1. My family live in a watery kingdom under a southern sky. 2. I have a letter ready to send them, 3. But the southward-flying geese won't go beyond Hengyang; 4. The brown dog who can carry letters hasn't the strength to get there; 5. And the fish are too stupid to be trusted. 6. How long must I wait while communications between us are continuously blocked?

---

* The figures in brackets indicate the number of stressed syllables in the line.

B
YUCHI THRICE TAKES THE LANCE

1. 誰似俺出氣力功臣不氣長   (7)
Shui si an / CHU QI li / GONG CHEN / BU QI CHANG
Who like me / putting out effort / meritorious subject /
unlucky

2. 想當時反在晉陽   (5)
XIANG dang SHI / FAN / zai JIN YANG
When I think of that time / rebel / in Jinyang

3. 若不是唐元帥少年有紀網   (7)
Ruo bu shi / TANG YUAN SHUAI / SHAO nian /
YOU JI GANG
If it weren't for / Tang marshal / young years / have
principles

4. 義伏了徐茂公   (5)
YI / FU liao / XU MAO GONG
By justice / won submission of / Xu Maogong

5. 禮說了褚遂良   (5)
LI / SHUI liao / CHU SUI LIANG
By courtesy / talked round / Chu Suiliang

6. 智降了蘇定方   (5)
ZHI / XIANG liao / SU DING FANG
By knowledge / caused surrender of / Su Dingfang

1. It would be hard to find a distinguished officer who had used so much effort to so little effect as me. 2. I think of the time when we raised the standard of rebellion in Jingyang: 3. Only our Tang commander, who even in his youth showed himself to be a man of principle, 4. Could have won over Xu Maogong by his sense of justice, 5. Or talked Chu Suiliang into an agreement by his courtesy, 6. Or brought about Su Dingfang's surrender by his superior intelligence.

C
A STUDIED INSULT

1. 怎不教我登時殺壞他 (7)
   Zen bu JIAO WO / DENG SHI / SHA HUAI TA
   Why not let me / straight away / kill him

2. 便教我做活佛，活佛怎定奪 (5)
   Bian jiao wo / ZUO huo FO / huo fo ZEN DING DUO
   Even if I / decide to be a living Buddha / living Buddha how safe

3. 咱將他來意兒早識破 (7)
   Za / JIANG TA LAI YI er / ZAO SHI PO
   I / his reason for coming / already see through

4. 他道是逞不盡口內詞 (5)
   Ta dao shi / CHENG bu JIN / KOU NEI CI
   He reckons that / before finished saying / words in his mouth

5. 卻教咱案不住心上火 (5)
   Que jiao za / AN bu ZHU / XIN SHANG HUO
   He'll make me / unable to repress / fire on my heart

6. 咱如今先備下這殺人刀門扇似闊 (5)
   Za ru jin / xian BEI xia / zhe SHA ren DAO / MEN shan si KUO
   I have now / in readiness prepared / this murderous sword / door wide open

1. Perhaps I should kill him straight away. 2. If I act the Merciful Buddha and let him live, I shan't be very safe. 3. I think I know why he's come: 4. He thinks that even before he's finished saying what he's got to say 5. He will be able to make me lose my temper (so that I become incoherent and can't argue properly and he will be able to outwit me.) *At this point there is some spoken dialogue as he summons guards to stand inside the tent with drawn swords.* 6. Now, with swords ready on either side of it ready to kill him, my door opens wide in welcome.

D
SNOW IN SUMMER

1. 莫不是前世裏燒香不到頭   (7)

   Mo bu shi / QIAN SHI li / SHAO XIANG / BU DAO TOU

   Could it be that / in a former life / burned incense / not to the end

2. 今也波生招禍尤   (5)

   JIN ye bo SHENG / ZHAO HUO YOU

   This life / bring on calamities

3. 勸今人早將來世修   (7)

   Quan JIN REN / ZAO / JIANG LAI SHI XIU

   I urge people today / in advance / future life cultivate

4. 我將這婆侍養   (5)

   WO / JIANG zhe PO / SHI YANG

   I / this old woman / wait on her needs

5. 我將這服孝守   (5)

   WO / JIANG zhe FU XIAO / SHOU

   I / this mourning / observe

6. 我言詞須應口   (5)

   Wo YAN CI / XU YING KOU

   My words / must correspond with mouth

1. It must be because in a past life I failed to fulfil some vow.
2. That I have brought all these misfortunes on myself in this one.
3. People today would be well advised to make preparations for the life to come. 4. I shall continue to support my old mother-in-law; 5. I shall continue to go on wearing mourning for my husband. 6. I have given my word, and so I shall keep it.

E
RIOT IN THE REQUIEM

1. 只疑是銀河落九天 (7)
ZHI YI shi / YIN HE / LUO JIU TIAN
Just wonder is it / Milky Way / fallen from nine heavens

2. 淵泉雲外懸 (5)
YUAN QUAN / YUN WAI / XUAN
Source / beyond the clouds / hangs

3. 入東洋不離此徑穿 (7)
Ru DONG YANG / BU LI CI JING / CHUAN
Entering eastern ocean / not leave this course / run through

4. 滋洛陽千種花 (5)
Zi / LUO YANG / QIAN ZHONG HUA
Watering / Loyang / thousand kinds of flowers

5. 潤梁園萬頃田 (5)
Run / LIANG YUAN / WAN QING TIAN
Irrigating / Liang Garden / myriad acre fields

6. 也曾泛浮槎到日月邊 (5)
Ye ceng fan / FU CHA / dao RI YUE BIAN
Also once floated / raft / to sun and moon side

1. You'd almost think the Milky Way had fallen out of the ninefold sky 2. From its source way up beyond the clouds. 3. From here it runs on this same course all the way till it enters the Eastern Sea. 4. On the way it waters the flowers of Loyang, 5. And irrigates the Liang Garden's myriad acres. 6. Once a raft floated on its waters upwards to the neighbourhood of the sun and moon.

F
THE LOVER'S SICKNESS

1. 方信道才子佳人信有之   (7)

    Fang xin dao / CAI ZI JIA REN / XIN YOU ZHI

    Now at last believe / story-book lovers / really do exist

2. 紅娘看時有些乖性兒   (5)

    Hong niang KAN SHI / you xie / GUAI XING ER*

    When I, Hongniang, consider / there's something / a bit
    weird about them

3. 則怕有情人不遂心也似此   (7)

    Ze pa / YOU qing REN / bu SUI XIN / YE SI CI

    I suppose / people of feeling / when things aren't going
    their way / do behave like this

4. 他害的有些抹媚   (5)

    TA HAI de / YOU xie / MO MEI

    He's already suffering / from a certain amount of / infatuation

5. 我遭著沒三思   (5)

    WO ZAO zhe / MEI SAN SI

    If I tackle him / too abruptly

6. 一納頭安排著憔悴死   (5)

    Yi na tou / AN PAI zhe / QIAO CUI SI

    Melancholy / may cause him / to die of grief

1. Now I believe there really are people like those heroes and heroines of romance. 2. When I look at them, there is definitely something rather weird about this couple. 3. I suppose this is how people with sensibility do behave when things aren't going their way. 4. It's a sort of lover's madness he's suffering from. 5. If I tackle him too suddenly 6. The melancholy may take a turn for the worse and cause him to die of grief.

---

* Contemporary (Yuan) pronunciation NYI. As elsewhere, line 2 rhymes with lines 1, 3, 5 and 6.

G
DREAMING OF YINGYING

1. 我則索倚定門兒手托腮   (7)
   Wo ze suo / YI DING MEN ER / SHOU TUO SAI
   I'll just have to / lean close by the door / hand supporting
   my cheek

2. 好著我難猜來也那不來   (5)
   Hao zhao wo NAN CAI / LAI ye NA bu LAI
   Really hard for me to guess / come or won't come

3. 夫人行料應難離側   (7)
   FU ren HANG / LIAO YING / NAN LI CE*
   From her lady mother / I suppose / hard to leave the side

4. 望得人眼欲穿   (5)
   WANG de / REN YAN / YU CHUAN
   Gazing till / one's eyes / likely to bore holes

5. 想得人心越窄   (5)
   XIANG de / REN XIN / YUE ZHAI
   Longing till / one's heart / even more contracted

6. 多管是冤家不自在   (5)
   Duo guan shi / YUAN JIA / BU ZI ZAI
   Probably / my beloved enemy / isn't well

   1. I shall just have to lean by the door, chin on hand, waiting. 2. It's
hard to guess: will she come or not? 3. I suppose it's hard for her to get
away from her mother. 4. I gaze till my eyes could almost pierce
through to her, 5. I yearn till my heart contracts with painful longing.
6. Dear enemy! I suppose she doesn't come because she's ill.

---

* Contemporary pronunciation CAI. See note on F2.

H
THE HOVEL IN A HOLE

1. 豈不聞有福之人不在忙   (7)
   Qi bu wen / YOU FU ZHI REN / BU ZAI MANG
   Haven't you heard / prosperous people / don't get there by hurrying

2. 我這裏參也波詳   (5)*
   WO zhe LI / CAN ye bo XIANG
   I here / reflect

3. 心自想平地一聲雷振響   (7)
   Xin zi xiang / PING DI / YI SHENG LEI ZHEN XIANG
   I consider in my heart / on the level earth / there is a sudden clap of thunder

4. 朝為田舍郎   (5)
   ZHAO / WEI / TIAN SHE LANG
   Morning / being / a peasant in a cottage

5. 暮登天子堂   (5)
   MU / DENG / TIAN ZI TANG
   Evening / mounting to / emperor's palace hall

6. 可不道寒門生將相   (5)
   Ke bu dao / HAN MEN / SHENG JIANG XIANG
   Don't they say / humble families / breed generals, statesmen

1. It's well-known that good fortune doesn't come in a hurry. 2. I've considered this carefully. 3. I've thought how suddenly, out of the blue, there can be a sudden clap of thunder, 4. And someone who was a humble peasant in the morning 5. That same evening can find himself mounting the steps of the Emperor's palace. 6. Don't they speak of humble hearths as the breeding ground of our greatest soldiers and statesmen?

---

* *Ye bo* is the equivalent of one full beat. See p. 106.

I
THE HIBISCUS PAVILION

1. 恰做了十謁朱門九不開   (7)
   Qia zuo liao / SHI YE ZHU MEN / JIU BU KAI
   This is like/"Ten times visiting rich men's doors/and
   nine won't open"

2. 書齋好幽哉，不曾有俗客來   (5)
   Shu zhai / HAO you ZAI / bu ceng you / SU KE LAI
   The study/is very secluded/there haven't been/vulgar
   guests coming

3. 將舊幃屏兒扇兒窗下擺   (7)
   Jiang JIU WEI PING er SHAN er / CHUANG XIA / BAI
   An old folding screen/under the window/arranged

4. 戀蝴蝶床榻兒窄   (5)
   LIAN HU die / CHUANG TA er / ZHAI
   Delighting in butterflies/bed/narrow

5. 夢梅花紙帳兒矮   (5)
   MENG MEI hua / ZHI ZHANG er / AI
   Dreaming of plum-blossom/paper/short

6. 你正是成人好不自在   (5)
   Ni zheng shi / CHENG REN / HAO bu ZI ZAI
   You really are/making yourself/very uncomfortable

1. Here's a fine case of "knocking in vain on great men's doors"!
2. How secluded this study seems! I'm sure no vulgar guests come this
way. 3. He's put an old folding-screen up below the window. 4. The
bed's a bit narrow for mating butterflies. 5. That paper's not the right
size for plum-flower fantasies. 6. You certainly aren't doing much to
make yourself comfortable.

LINE-BY-LINE COMPARISON

LINE 1

A. 俺家在南天水國居
An JIA ZAI NAN TIAN SHUI GUO JU

B. 誰似俺出氣力功臣不氣長
Shui si an CHU QI li GONG CHEN BU QI CHANG

C. 怎不教我登時殺壞他
Zen bu JIAO WO DENG SHI SHA HUAI TA

D. 莫不是前世裏燒香不到頭
Mo bu shi QIAN SHI li SHAO XIANG BU DAO TOU

E. 只疑是銀河落九天
ZHI YI shi YIN HE LUO JIU TIAN

F. 方信道才子佳人信有之
Fang xin dao CAI ZI JIA REN XIN YOU ZHI

G. 我則索倚定門兒手托腮
Wo ze suo YI DING MEN ER SHOU TUO SAI

H. 豈不聞有福之人不在忙
Qi bu wen YOU FU ZHI REN BU ZAI MANG

I. 恰做了十謁朱門九不開
Qia zuo liao SHI YE ZHU MEN JIU BU KAI

LINE 2

A. 就兒裏非無尺素書
JIU er LI fei wu CHI SU SHU

B. 想當時反在晉陽
XIANG dang SHI FAN zai JIN YANG

C. 便教我做活佛，活佛怎定奪
Bian jiao wo ZUO huo FO, huo fo ZEN DING DUO

D. 今也波生招禍尤
JIN ye bo SHENG ZHAO HUO YOU

E. 淵泉雲外懸
YUAN QUAN YUN WAI XUAN

F. 紅娘看時有些乖性兒
Hong niang KAN SHI you xie GUAI XING ER

G. 好著我難猜來也那不來
Hao zhao wo NAN CAI LAI ye NA bu LAI

H. 我這裏參也波詳
WO zhe LI CAN ye bo XIANG

I. 書齋好幽哉，不曾有俗客來
Shu zhai HAO you ZAI, bu ceng you SU KE LAI

LINE 3

A. 奈衡陽不傳鴻雁羽

Nai HENG YANG BU CHUAN HONG YAU YU

B. 若不是唐元帥少年有紀網

Ruo bu shi TANG YUAN SHUAI SHAO nian YOU JI GANG

C. 咱將他來意兒早識破

Za JIANG TA LAI YI er ZAO SHI PO

D. 勸今人早將來世修

Quan JIN REN ZAO JIANG LAI SHI XIU

E. 入東洋不離此徑穿

Ru DONG YANG BU LI CI JING CHUAN

F. 則怕有情人不遂心也似此

Ze pa YOU qing REN bu SUI XIN YE SI CI

G. 夫人行料應難離側

FU ren HANG LIAO YING NAN LI CE

H. 心自想平地一聲雷振響

Xin zi xiang PING DI YI SHENG LEI ZHEN XIANG

I. 將舊幃屏兒扇兒窗下擺

Jiang JIU WEI PING er SHAN er CHUANG XIA BAI

LINE 4

A. 黃犬又筋力疲
   HUANG QUAN you JIN LI PI

B. 義伏了徐茂公
   YI FU liao XU MAO GONG

C. 他道是逞不盡口內詞
   Ta dao shi CHENG bu JIN KOU NEI CI

D. 我將這婆侍養
   WO JIANG zhe PO SI YANG

E. 滋洛陽千種花
   Zi LUO YANG QIAN ZHONG HUA

F. 他害的有些抹媚
   TA HAI de YOU xie MO MEI

G. 望得人眼欲穿
   WANG de REN YAN YU CHUAN

H. 朝為田舍郎
   ZHAO WEI TIAN SHE LANG

I. 戀蝴蝶床榻兒窄
   LIAN HU die CHUANG TA er ZHAI

LINE 5

A. 錦鱗又性格愚
JIN LIN you XING GE YU

B. 禮説了褚遂良
LI SHUI liao CHU SUI LIANG

C. 卻教咱案不住心上火
Que jiao za AN bu ZHU XIN SHANG HUO

D. 我將這服孝守
WO JIANG zhe FU XIAO SHOU

E. 潤梁園萬頃田
Run LIANG YUAN WAN QING TIAN

F. 我遭著沒三思
WO ZAO zhe MEI SAN SI

G. 想得人心越窄
XIANG de REN XIN YUE ZHAI

H. 暮登天子堂
MU DENG TIAN ZI TANG

I. 夢梅花紙帳兒矮
MENG MEI hua ZHI ZHANG er AI

LINE 6

A. 幾遍家待相通常間阻
Ji bian jia dai XIANG TONG CHANG JIAN ZU

B. 智降了蘇定方
ZHI XIANG liao SU DING FANG

C. 咱如今先備下這殺人刀門扇似闊
Za ru jin xian BEI xia zhe SHA ren DAO MEN shan si KUO

D. 我言詞須應口
Wo YAN CI XU YING KOU

E. 也曾泛浮槎到日月邊
Ye ceng fan FU CHA dao RI YUE BIAN

F. 一納頭安排著憔悴死
Yi na tou AN PAI zhe QIAO CUI SI

G. 多管是冤家不自在
Duo guan shi YUAN JIA BU ZI ZAI

H. 可不道寒門生將相
Ke bu dao HAN MEN SHENG JIANG XIANG

I. 你正是成人好不自在
Ni zheng shi CHENG REN HAO bu ZI ZAI

How words are matched to melody in Chinese vocal music is a matter best left for Chinese musicologists to explain. In the case of Yuan *zaju*, since the music is virtually lost, one can only state the obvious: that the Yuan playwrights were writing lyrics that they knew could be accommodated by the music that they were writing for; and that the music was suited to the language in which they wrote.

In the examples of the same *Tian xia le* lyric collected above there is a wide variation in the lengths of corresponding lines. The number of syllables in line 1 varies between eight and eleven, that in line 2 between five and eleven, that in line 3 between eight and eleven, that in lines 4 and 5 between five and nine, and that in line 6 between six and fourteen — the longest example nearly two-and-a-half times as long as the shortest!

Classical Chinese poetry is syllabic, with lines of fixed length. The number of syllables in each line, whether the poem is in lines of regular length throughout or in lines of different lengths arranged in fixed patterns, is a defining feature of Chinese prosody and the irregularities of *zaju* lyrics are ascribed to the presence of *chenzi* or "padding words", often defined as "words or phrases external to the prescribed lyrical metre".

From as early as the eighth century Chinese poets writing in the style of the popular ballad have sometimes interpolated a few words "outside the metre" for the sake of vividness. For example, Du Fu, in his "Ballad of the Army Carts", suddenly, in the middle of a regular sequence of seven-syllable lines, interpolates the words 君不聞 *Jun bu wen*: "Haven't you heard that ..." before the beginning of a line, which exactly parallels a common practice of Yuan lyricists. H1 豈不聞 *Qi bu wen*: "Surely you've heard that ..." is virtually the same phrase, and there are no less than eighteen other examples of phrases of three words or more interpolated "outside the metre" (whatever that meant in musical terms) just in the nine lyrics cited in this Appendix.

But though these prefatory, "external" phrases seem to correspond with the traditional definition of *chenzi* , discounting them metrically is often insufficient to uncover the underlying rhythmic pattern of the line. I think this is because the language which is the medium of these lyrics is a vernacular in which stress accent is increasingly important and the old-fashioned obsession with syllable-count irrelevant.

Not that syllable-count does not sometimes play a significant part in the prosody. Consider I1: 恰做了十謁朱門九不開. If you discount the "padding words" 恰做了 ("This is just like ..." or "Here's a fine case of ..."), what follows looks like a line from a seven-syllable classical poem. As a matter of fact it is. It is the first line of a quatrain in regular heptasyllablic verse by Lü Mengzheng (946–1011), the historical person who is the leading male character in H. The line was evidently popular, because it is used by another playwright, Ma Zhiyuan (馬致遠) in a play called "The Stele" (荐福碑) where a poor scholar teaching in a village school is explaining why he gave up trying to improve his prospects by using letters of introduction to important people given him by a well-placed friend because of his failure to gain access to the addressees. In this case the line is 況兼今日十謁朱門九不開 with different *chenzi* "outside the metre", but more often the rhythmic pattern is arrived at by discounting unstressed syllables inside it.

Yuan lyrics contain an abundance of the nominal and verbal suffixes, conjunctions, prepositions, and so forth, which classical verse normally avoided. They are almost invariably unstressed. *Er* 兒, the commonest nominal suffix, in the modern dialect of Peking elides with the noun to form what is virtually a monosyllable, so that *men-er* "door" becomes *mer*. Examples in these lyrics can be found in C3 來意兒 *lai yi er*, I3 幃屏兒 *wei ping er* 扇兒 *shan er*, I4 床榻兒 *chuang ta er*, I5 紙帳兒 *zhi zhang er*. Examples of verbal suffixes can be found in F5 遭著 *zao zhe*, F6 安排著 *an pai zhe*, F4 害的 *hai de*, G4 望得 *wang de*, G5 想得 *xiang de*, B4 服了 *fu liao*, B5 説了 *shui liao*, B6 降了 *xiang liao*.

The negative 不 *bu* is frequently unstressed: F3 不遂心 *bu sui xin*, C4 逞不盡 *cheng bu jin*, C5 案不住 *an bu zhu*, I6 好不自在 *hao bu zi zai*.

For examples of unstressed prepositions see 在 *zai* in B2 在晉陽 *zai Jinyang*; 到 *dao* in E6 到日月邊 *dao ri yue bian* and 裏 *li* in D1 前世裏 *qian shi li*; 又 *you* in A4 又筋力疲 *you jin li pi* and A5 又性格愚 *you xing ge yu* is an unstressed conjunction and 這 *zhe* in D4 這婆 *zhe po* and D5 這服孝 *zhe fu xiao* is an unstressed demonstrative.

However, such words are not invariably unstressed. They may sometimes be stressed if the rhythm requires it. Take 兒 *er* in G1, for example: 倚定門兒手托腮. Wang Shifu evidently liked this line sufficiently to use it again in another play. In both cases it's quite clearly meant to be treated as a heptasyllabic line. Another example is 在 *zai* in A1: 家在南天水國居 where it clearly has equal metrical value with the other syllables of the heptasyllabic line.

Sometimes a syllable is unstressed in a compound word of two or more syllables, as regularly happens in Modern Chinese. For example, in B1 氣力 *qi li*, B3 少年 *shao nian*, F4 有些 *you xie*, I4 蝴蝶 *hu die* and I5 梅花 *mei hua*, the second syllable is unstressed; while in C6 殺人刀 *sha ren dao* and F3 有情人 *you qing ren* only the first and last syllables are stressed.

By counting stress accents rather than syllables it soon becomes clear that the metrical pattern of a *Tian xia le* lyric is 7:?:7:5:5:5, with line 2 remaining problematic. From E2 it would appear that line 2 should also have five stressed syllables, like lines 4–6; but a glance at the longer examples in C, F, G and I make this look almost impossible.

A possible solution might be that one half of the line is spoken, not sung, and therefore "outside the metre" (lyrics are frequently interrupted when a singer stops midway in his singing, speaks a line or two, and then continues the aria where he had left off). This is unlikely, though, because in all these lines there is an internal rhyme, for example, in G2 難猜 *nan cai* rhymes with 來也那不來 *lai ye na bu lai* and therefore must belong to the sung part of the lyric.

An alternative solution which might seem more likely, because it would account for the internal rhyme, is that the musical phrase that came between the singing of lines 1 and 3 could (optionally) be repeated, so that line 2 in C, G and I is really not one line but two:

好著我難猜 *hao zhao wo nan cai*
來也那不來 *lai ye na bu lai*

A possible objection to this solution, however, is that the first half of F2 has only four stressed syllables and that E2, in which there is internal rhyme, divides into two sections of only two and three syllables respectively. I think it may be in E2 that the key to this problem lies.

A *zaju* called "An Heir in His Old Age" (老生兒) by the playwright Wu Hanchen (武漢臣) exists in two versions, one of them a contemporary Yuan edition. There is a startling difference between the two versions of line 2 of the *Tian xia le* lyric in this play. One version has

興衰天數該
Xing shuai, tian shu gai

in the other version this becomes

問什麼興也波衰，總是那天數該
Wen shen mo xing ye bo shuai, zong shi na tian shu gai

Ye bo (也波) is a nonce-word frequently used in *zaju* lyrics. It is a bit like the meaningless refrains of English ballad: fa-la, diddle diddle, and so forth, but is used in a rather peculiar way. Almost invariably it is inserted between the two syllables of a normally indivisible compound word. There are examples of it in D2 and H2. *Jin sheng* (今生) means "this life" (as opposed to "former life"); *canxiang* (參詳) is a bisyllabic word meaning "reflect" or "consider". It is a bit like singing "post diddle man" for "postman" or "dust tra la bin" for "dustbin".

Here are a few examples from other plays:

(1) The first is from "The Golden Toy" (生金閣) by the author of "An Heir in His Old Age", Wu Hanchen:

自我也當也波初自窨付
Zi wo ye dang ye bo chu, zi yin fu
"Starting out with all this store of knowledge …"

This is a poor scholar, caught in a snowstorm while travelling to the capital with his wife to seek his fortune. (當初 means "at first", "in the beginning".) The key words are 當初, 自窨付 (*dang chu, zi yin fu*).

(2) From "Wu Yuan Plays the Flute" (伍員吹蕭) by Li Shouqing (李壽卿):

似這般傍也波徨，都只是為我行

Si zhe ban pang ye bo huang, dou zhi shi wei wo hang

"So much rushing around, all for my sake"

傍徨 *pang huang* means "going to and fro". The key words are 傍徨為我行 *pang huang wei wo hang*.

(3) The third example is from a *zaju* called "Unidentified Corpse" (不認尸) by a playwright called Wang Zhongwen (王仲文):

哎！你個兒也波那，休學這令史咱

Ai! Ni ge er ye bo na, xiu xue zhe ling shi za

A mother scratching a living from the soil with her two sons exhorts the educated one to aspire to something higher than a pen-pushing clerkship.

"Oh my boy! Don't study to be a government clerk!"

Ni ge er ye bo na (oh my boy) reduces to just "*er*", since the "*na*" in "*er na*", though it is given stress here, has only a vocative function and no meaning. The key words are 兒那 *er na* and 令史咱 *ling shi za*.

From these examples it is easy to see now E2 could be expanded into a line of many more syllables yet still have only five stresses, in the same way that the five syllables in the line from the first version of "An Heir in His Old Age" were expanded into the thirteen syllables of the longer version.

If *chenzi* are thought of as unstressed syllables which are in some sense "excluded" from the rhythmic beat, nonce expressions like *ye bo* have been deliberately inserted because the musical score requires them.

In the folk opera "The White-haired Girl" first publicly performed in Peking in 1949, the opening lyric begins with the words

北風吹   *bei feng chui*   The north wind blows
雪花飄   *xue hua piao*   The snowflakes swirl ...

Metrically these could be described as the first two lines of a 3:3:7 or 3:3:4:3 stanza; but what was actually sung was

Bei feng na ge chui
Xue hua na ge piao

where the meaningless *na ge* is used, just like *ye bo* in the Yuan plays, as a filler to meet the rhythmic requirement of the music.

The internal rhyme often occurring in the second line of *Tian xia le* already suggests that the line divides into two parts, with two strong beats in the first half and three in the second:

| | tum   tum : tum tum tum | (E2) |
| or | tum titi tum : tum tum tum | (D2) |

This could equally well be expressed in musical notation:

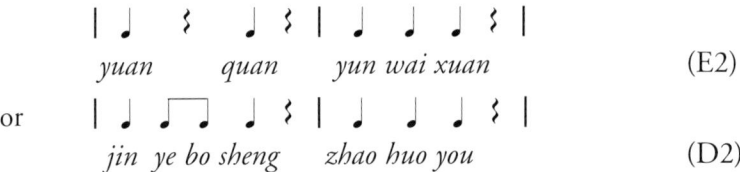

| | *yuan   quan   yun wai xuan* | (E2) |
| or | *jin ye bo sheng   zhao huo you* | (D2) |

In the case of H2, the *ye bo* would represent two half-beats occupying the place of one full beat:

tum tee tum : tum titi tum

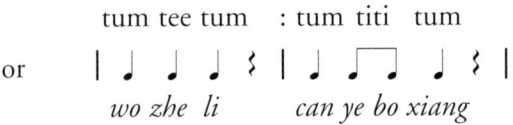

or   *wo zhe li   can ye bo xiang*

and G2 would be

nan   cai   lai ye na bu lai

As well as writing lyrics for the theatre, many *zaju*-writers also composed song-lyrics which the talented inhabitants of the brothels could sing to their own or others' accompaniment for the entertainment of their clients. Perhaps because of the clients' preferences, the selection of tunes they set them to was somewhat different from that used for the *zaju* lyrics, but the way they use *chenzi* in them seems pretty much the same.

One of them was the playwright Ma Zhiyuan (馬致遠), the most poetical of the *zaju*-writers, as the Ming aficionado Zang Maoxun (臧懋循) recognised by placing his "Autumn in the Han Palace" (漢宮秋) at the head of the selection of 100 Yuan *zaju*, his *Yuan qu xuan* (元曲選), published in 1616 — the year that Shakespeare died — which has long been the most popular and accessible anthology of this literature.

Ma Zhiyuan was a very prolific song-writer and often wrote a whole series of short lyrics to be sung to the same tune. In such cases it becomes much easier to grasp the overall rhythmic pattern of the lyrics by observing variations in their corresponding lines than it was in the case of the *zaju* lyrics.

In thirty-one of the five-line lyrics he wrote to the tune of *Shou*

---

* If the first half of the second line of *Tian xia le* is thought of as having two strong beats with a weak beat or its equivalent (a rest or two half-beats) in between, viz. *tum tee tum* in A, B, C, H and I; *tum – tum* in E, F, G; and *tum titi tum* in D; then it would perhaps be more accurate to describe the pattern of line 2 as the equivalent of six beats divided in two groups of three, rather than as five stressed syllables with a caesura after the second. With this material the confusion between metre and musical beat seems unavoidable.

yang qu (壽陽曲) the rhythmic pattern is 3:3:7:7:7.* Nearly all the variations occur in line 4. The fourth lines of two of these songs are as follows:

似鴛鴦失群迷伴侶

(Si) yuan yang shi qun mi ban lü

Like a duck cut off from the flock that has lost its mate

No. 3 平沙落雁**

and

四圍山一竿殘照裏

Si wei shan (yi gan) can zhao li

On the mountains all round one rod of setting sun shines

No. 1 山市晴嵐

---

* The 3:3:7 rhythm seems to be universal. Its equivalent in Western musical notation is

| ♩ ♩ ♪ | ♩ ♩ ♪ | ♩ ♪ ♪ ♪ | ♩ ♩ ♪ |

It appears in the "Music of a Thousand Autumns" (千秋樂) which was first performed at the Tang court in A.D. 728 and in English children's rhymes:

> Bounce me high,
> Bounce me low,
> Bounce me up to Jericho.

or

> This old man
> He plays one
> He plays knick-knack on my drum.

In origin it may have been a marching rhythm — a speeded-up version of the drill-sergeant's familiar "left – left –, left, right, left". In the variant form:

| ♩ ♩ ♪ ⅄ | ♩ ♩ ♪ ⅄ | ♩ ♩ ♪ ♪ | ♩ ♩ ♪ ⅄ |
L R L (R)   L R L (R)   L R L R   L R L (R)

each bar represents four steps, while the rests at the end of the first, second and fourth bars represent the intake of breath.

** This, and the example quoted below, come from a series of Ma's thirty-one *Shou yang qu* lyrics which were inspired by landscapes of Hunanese lake and river scenery — now unfortunately lost — painted by an eleventh-century artist called Song Di (宋迪). The titles are the titles of the paintings.

In the first example *si* "like" precedes the rhythmic line and can unhesitatingly be described as a *chenzi*; but in the second example *yi gan* "one rod" (i.e. very low: the sun is said to be "three rods high" between 8 and 9 a.m.) *could* be explained as one stressed syllable and one monosyllabic *chenzi*, and a text which distinguished stressed from unstressed syllables might well print one or another (but not both) of the characters as unstressed to make it clear that this is a seven-stress line. In fact, though, the two syllables should probably be thought of as two half-beats and equivalent to one whole beat, which, using Western musical notation and writing in common (4/4) time, would be:

| ♩ ♩ ♩ ♫ | ♩ ♩ ♩ ♩ |

si wei shan yi gan can zhao li

If it was not metre that writers like Ma had in mind when they composed their lyrics but what the Chinese call *ban yan* (板眼) or musical "beat", it would follow that no word or compound or phrase could be said to have had a fixed metrical value. Many words — particles, suffixes and the like — were *usually* unstressed, but could on occasion be stressed if the musical beat required it. Consider this song — No. 17 from the group of thirty-one *Shou yang qu* lyrics:

1. 人千里　　　　　　　*Ren qian li*
2. 愁萬縷　　　　　　　*Chou wan lü*
3. 望不斷野煙汀樹　　　*Wang bu duan ye yan ting shu*
4. 一會價上心來沒是處　*Yi hui (jia) shang xin (lai) mei shi chu*
5. 恨不得待跨鸞歸去　　*Hen (bu) de dai kua luan gui qu*

Hundreds of miles away
Thousands of sorrows
Gazing endlessly at the meadow mist and the waterside trees
A sudden pang assails my heart
And I wish I could mount on a phoenix and fly back there

Wang bu duan, lit. "gaze-not-breaking" in line 3 and *hen bu de*, lit. "regret-not-getting" in line 5 are grammatically equivalent and would normally have the same pattern of stressed and unstressed syllables, viz. *wàng bu duàn* and *hèn bu dè* (cf. C4 and C5 in the *Tian xia le* examples above); yet *wang bu duan* in line 3 clearly counts as three whole beats and *hen bu de* in line 5 as two:

In a group of fifteen lyrics all written to the tune of *Bo bu duan* (撥 不斷) in which the pattern is 3:3:7:7:7:4 (six lines) the variations nearly all occur in the sixth line, with *chenzi* of between two and four syllables *preceding* the rhythmic line. Thus, in line 6 of Song No. 3:

不如醉了還醉

Bu ru zui liao huan zui

Better get drunk and then get drunk again

bu ru is almost certainly to be thought of as a two-syllable *chenzi* "outside the line"; whereas in line 5 of Song No. 5:

到不如風雪銷金帳

Dao bu ru feng xue xiao jin zhang

But not as good as a gilded screen out in the wind and snow

the *chenzi* "outside the line" is almost certainly *dao* and *bu ru* counts as two full beats.

The music of Yuan *zaju* is lost and it is perhaps dangerous for a non-specialist to speculate about the way in which the words of the lyrics were sung, but I hope I have at least succeeded in demonstrating that without the music the metrical problems posed by this literature cannot be solved with any certainty.